MARLENE DIETRICH AND JOSEF VON STERNBERG

THE MOVIE GUIDE

Wisdom Twins Books, 2019
wisdomtwinsbooks.weebly.com

Text Copyright of Chris Wade, 2019

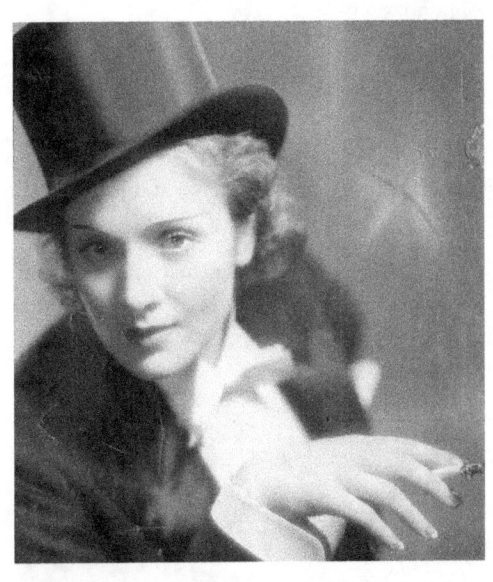

MARLENE DIETRICH AND JOSEF VON STERNBERG

THE MOVIE GUIDE

CONTENTS

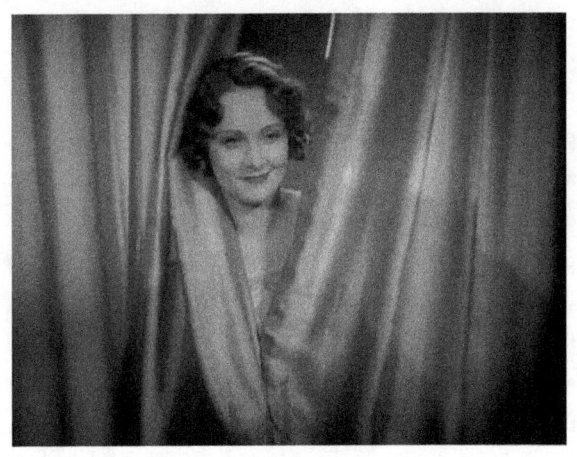

Introduction

This book, a tribute to the cinematic collaborations between Marlene Dietrich, one of the most enigmatic, iconic and striking icons from Hollywood's Golden era, and filmmaking giant Josef Von Sternberg, consists of an essay on their seven films together. Followed by an overview of Dietrich and the director's subsequent careers, the book explores in depth the masterpieces they made together - The Blue Angel, Morocco, Dishonoured, Shanghai Express, Blonde Venus, Scarlet Empress and The Devil is a Woman - and goes into the relationship - professional, personal and symbolic - between the two titans.

Very much a celebration of a one-off star and her maestro, a proto feminist who challenged sexual perceptions guided by a master of cinema, the book attempts to define what made Dietrich so popular, so unique and so loved in her time and beyond, as presented to us by von Sternberg. In many ways she was his obsession, his muse, the personification of his fantasies. But she was more than this too. In an age when stars cease to be mysterious, revealing all on tacky chat shows and reality TV freak fests, Dietrich sums up a bygone age of glamour and myth. Behind all this glitz though is an influential body of work on the screen. Fully understanding the many layers of the films she made with von Sternberg is not easy, and many film critics and historians have attempted to dissect the mystery of their collaboration. Some have perhaps leapt into psychoanalytical metaphors too deeply, but their efforts must be applauded.

This book is not an academic study of those seven films, but a celebration of them, and a reminder of their importance. The theories and conclusions drawn by others are discussed, but for the most part the book exists to illuminate these movies, some of which are overlooked these days, and highlight their timeless qualities.

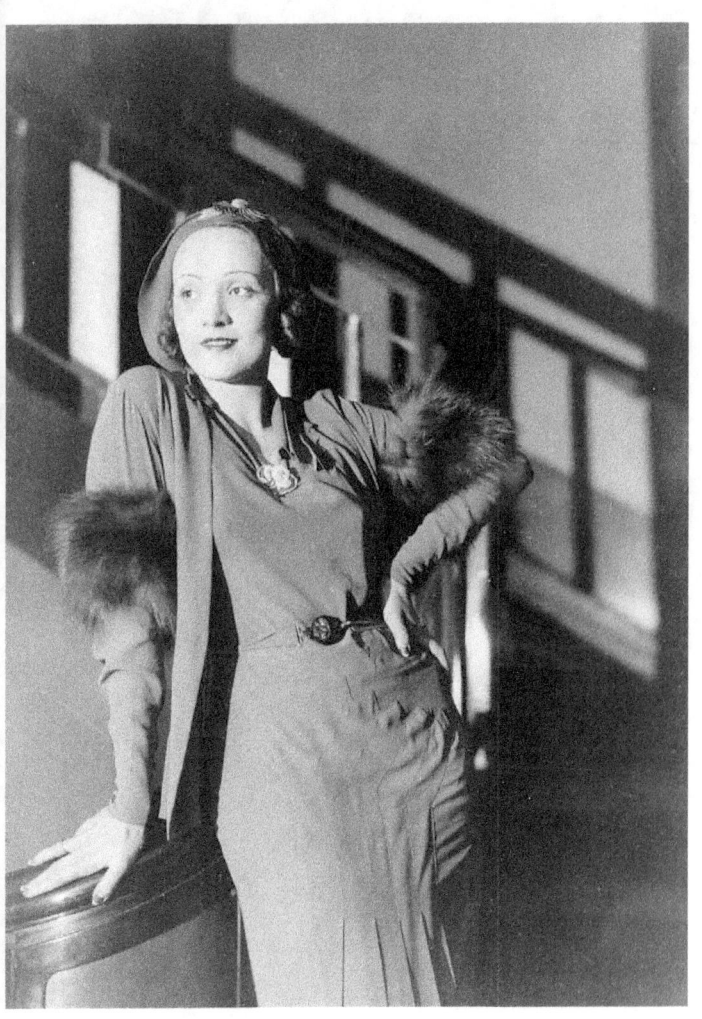

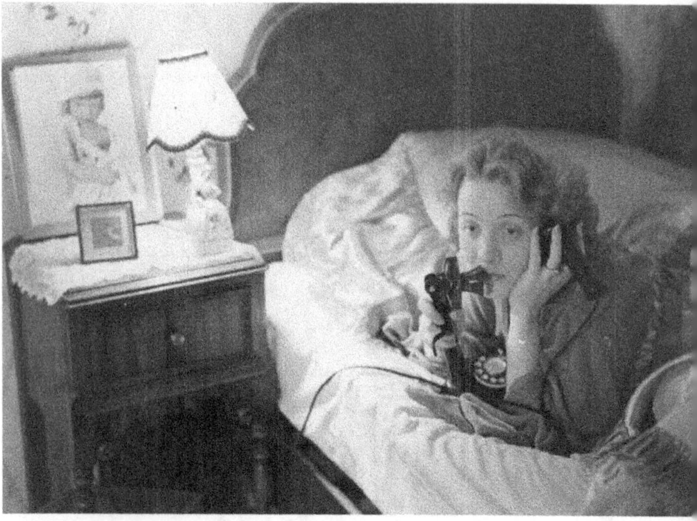

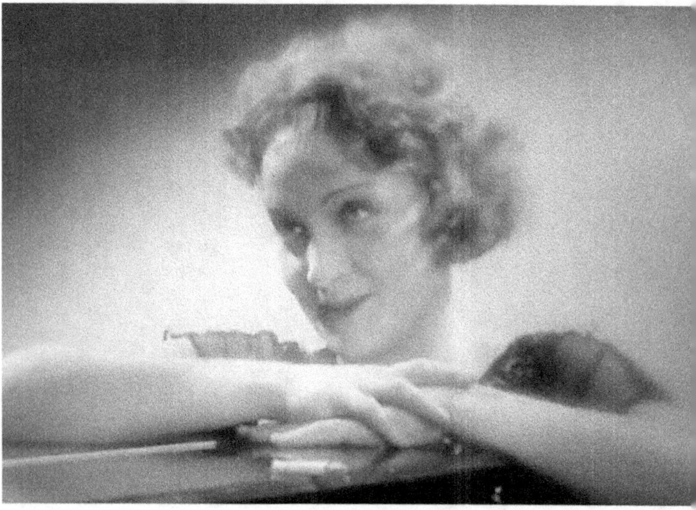

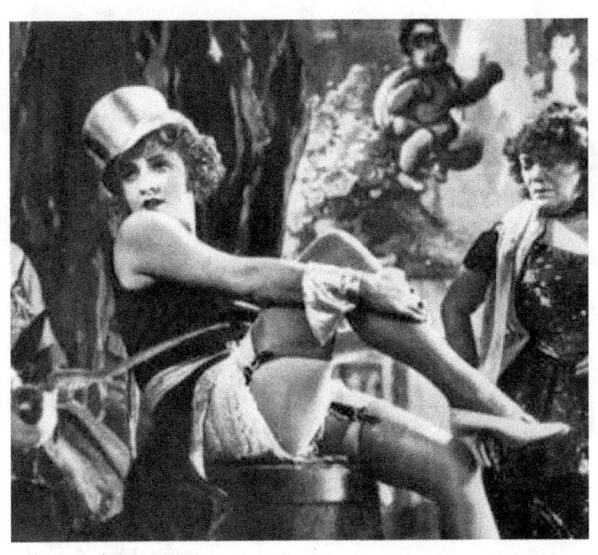

The Films of Marlene Dietrich and Josef von Sternberg

When exploring the film career of Marlene Dietrich, one is not accessing performances of extreme complexity, of subtle nuances and developments; one is simply enjoying heightened, stylised magic. Yes, Dietrich was a fabulous presence in the movies' golden era, but she was primarily a star of the screen (and stage of course), known for her glamour, larger than life exuberance and seductive appeal. But she was also in some truly brilliant films, and her range in them, still admittedly within the tight Dietrich parameter, was more varied than you might think.

These days, awareness of Dietrich varies. Older generations may remember her from when she was still around in the latter part of her screen career, popping up in brief cameos, many nods to her illustrious past; films buffs will know her retrospectively from her work with von Sternberg, those classic movies from the early thirties; younger generations may know the name and face but nothing else; while some, regrettably, will be absolutely clueless all together. This is, of course, inevitable, for the passage of time naturally sees that world famous legends soon fade away into obscurity. But some stars of the past deserve to stay relevant, not just for the work they left behind, but for their importance and impact on culture. For me, Dietrich is one of them.

Dietrich had already become a fixture of Germany's stage in the late twenties before her first worldwide film hit, 1930's The Blue Angel, made her a worldwide fascination. He and Marlene delicately crafted an image of enigmatic sensuality, not just by careful lighting and costume, but also presentation. Think, for instance, of when she first appears in 1932's Blonde

Venus, swimming naked in a lake, ogled by a group of men while she and her liberated friends frolic in the water. And who could forget the iconic moment in Shanghai Express, when she stands quietly, lit from above like a sensuous angel, smoking a cigarette with shaking hands. This picture, with Marlene as glowing goddess, has become one of the most enduring images of film's golden age.

Marlene captured the world's imagination through a deadly, enrapturing combination of factors, namely her glamour, her exotic classiness and her sex appeal. But Dietrich sensuality was not conveyed distastefully. Unlike today's female stars, who display their scantily clad bodies gratuitously just as present Hollywood requires, Marlene teased the audience, keeping herself at a certain distance but unveiling just enough of her mystique to hook the viewer from her first moment on the screen to the very last. Indeed, watching a Dietrich film is rather like being under a spell, and one cannot help but be seduced by the illusion created by both Dietrich and her director. As manufactured as her image may have been, one never gets the feeling of being tricked or duped; more hypnotised, won over.

The earliest part of Dietrich's on screen career is often forgotten these days, people choosing to believe that she exploded out of nowhere straight on to the screen in The Blue Angel, the role that made her a star. In reality, she had appeared in nearly twenty German silent films before Hollywood had even heard of her.

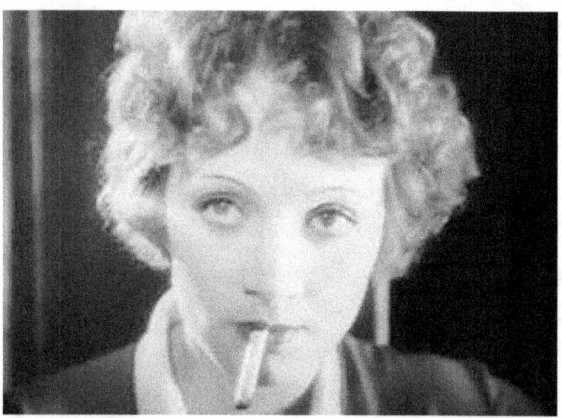

Granted, in such crackly, often gothic surroundings she is not the Marlene Dietrich we know from the golden period of thirties Hollywood, but in these unfairly overlooked movies, she harbours true star power and still commands the screen whenever she appears. The last two films she made before becoming a worldwide fascination were The Woman One Longs For and Ship of Lost Souls (both 1929), a pair of films which illuminated her unique air of mystery, setting her up for The Blue Angel.

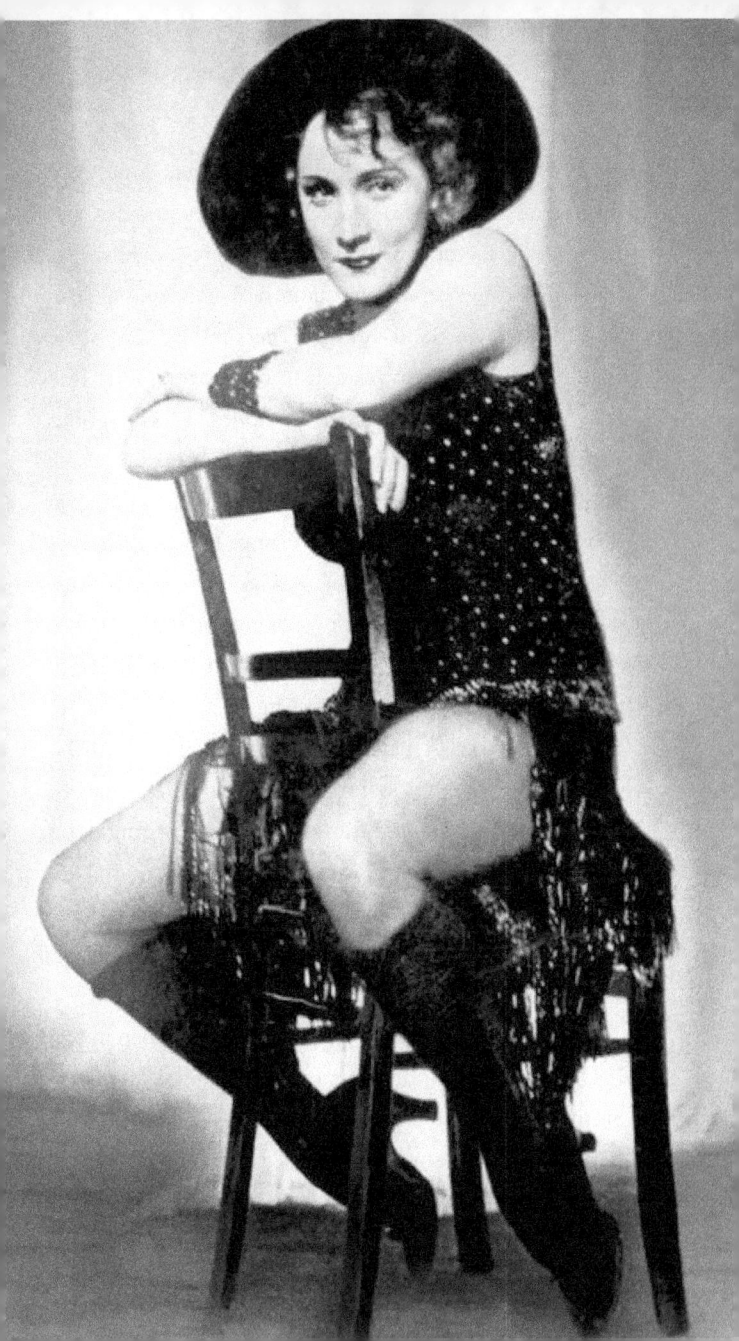

By 1929, Josef von Sternberg, the Austrian-American filmmaker, had directed a few successful movies for Paramount Pictures in the USA. Before establishing himself at the mammoth studio he'd had a colourful time in movie land, though not all of his film adventures were seen through to completion. First off, he'd had a brush with Mary Pickford, at one point Hollywood's most popular female star, but his proposed project for her was deemed too avant-garde, and after a stint at MGM, he was given the chance to direct Charlie Chaplin's A Woman of the Sea, a film which was destroyed after completion by Chaplin himself. Finally he found satisfaction, after a series of ill fated projects, in a run of films from 1928's The Last Command to 1929's The Case of Lena Smith. After he made 1929's Thunderbolt, he was approached by UFA, Germany's Paramount, to take on a film called The Blue Angel, to star Emil Jannings as Professor Immanuel Rath, an academic who suffers a tragic downfall when he becomes obsessed with a cabaret singer by the name of Lola-Lola.

Though it was to be a vehicle for Jennings, then at his height, the part of Lola-Lola was vital in von Sternberg's eyes, and for this part he needed to find the perfect actress, someone who could be sexy and appealing but do so without effort, without trying too hard to melt celluloid. When a young Marlene Dietrich auditioned, and in truth seemed half uninterested, von Sternberg saw in her the quality he had been searching for. Though no wide eyed innocent, she did look youthful and fresh. The director knew she was the only woman for the job, but the studio needed persuading, unsure that an unknown could carry such a film and convince in the central part.

Originally the part was going to go to Lucie Mannheim, a popular singer of the time, with both the studio and Jannings himself firm on this choice. Sternberg however found her unappealing, stating she did not have the necessary glamour to light up the screen. Other close calls were Brigitte Helm, who turned out to be busy, and Kathe Haack nearly signed, but any alternatives were binned when von Sternberg met Marlene and was bewitched by her peculiarity. When he met her in person for the first time he jumped in the air and shouted "It's Lola!" Haack was paid off and sent on her way, and Marlene, acting cool as a cucumber, took her place. In Josef's mind, Dietrich was vital for the film to succeed, and at one point told Heinrich Mann, the writer of the book the film was based on, that "the success of this film will be found in

15

the naked thighs of Miss Dietrich!" Eventually he got his way and Dietrich was cast. Seeing her potential, von Sternberg began to mould her to his liking.

The Blue Angel was actually shot twice, once in German and again with the actors speaking in English. Though both edits are excellent, one could say the songs are best heard in English, if only to put across the sincerity for English speaking viewers, while the movie itself is best seen in German, where the actors are truer to their roles and more natural/comfortable with their performances. In either form, the film succeeds not because of its loose story, nor even in the addictive tension between the ageing cuckold and his manipulative object of obsession, but because of Marlene herself. From the moment she appears, we are transfixed. Dietrich is at her most pure, her most fresh, plucked from the German stage and put forth to the world. She may have been von Sternberg's icon, gazing down at he and Emil Jennings from her pedestal, as if they were one and the same man (and in many ways, it has to be said, they are), but the power was in her hands.

The movie was a success in America, its release held up until January of 1931 when her first fully English speaking role in Morocco was unveiled. Her rise to fame was sudden and unexpected. Overnight it seemed that Dietrich was a sensation. Jannings is also brilliant in his role, going from respected academic to shameful clown, his descent into bedlam masterfully handled. Yet it is completely Dietrich's show; and how could it not be, when all the drive of the plot and the poor man's downfall rests on her sexuality, her power and ability to turn a man into mush. She is the seductress, and he is mere putty in her hands.

That is not to say Dietrich/Lola-Lola's manipulative characteristics make her an unsavoury character. It is very much not the case, because despite her torturing of the older man, she still seems innocent, though clearly being far from it. Others have voiced this opinion too, in particular the film critic Michael Aubriant, who wrote in 1966, "We probably all were victims of an illusion... the Marlene we rediscover is candour personified; a good-hearted little trouper, a bit overly romantic, perhaps, flattered by the attention of a pedant old enough to be her papa, dragging him along for four years like a ball and chain. Not a trace of malice. She prefers this clod to her gilded coxcombs. Of course she ends up cuckolding him, but almost against her own will. The idiot dies from it. Good riddance!"

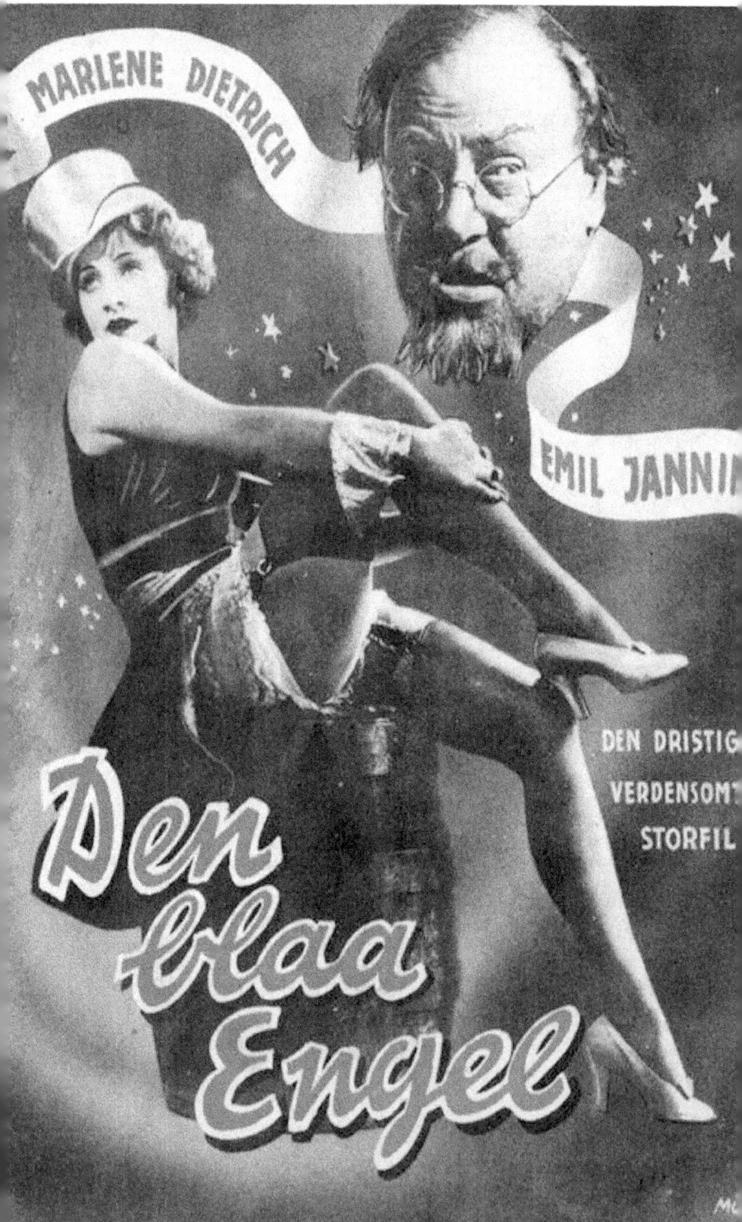

MARLENE DIETRICH
EMIL JANNI
DEN DRISTIG
VERDENSOMT
STORFIL
Den blaa Engel

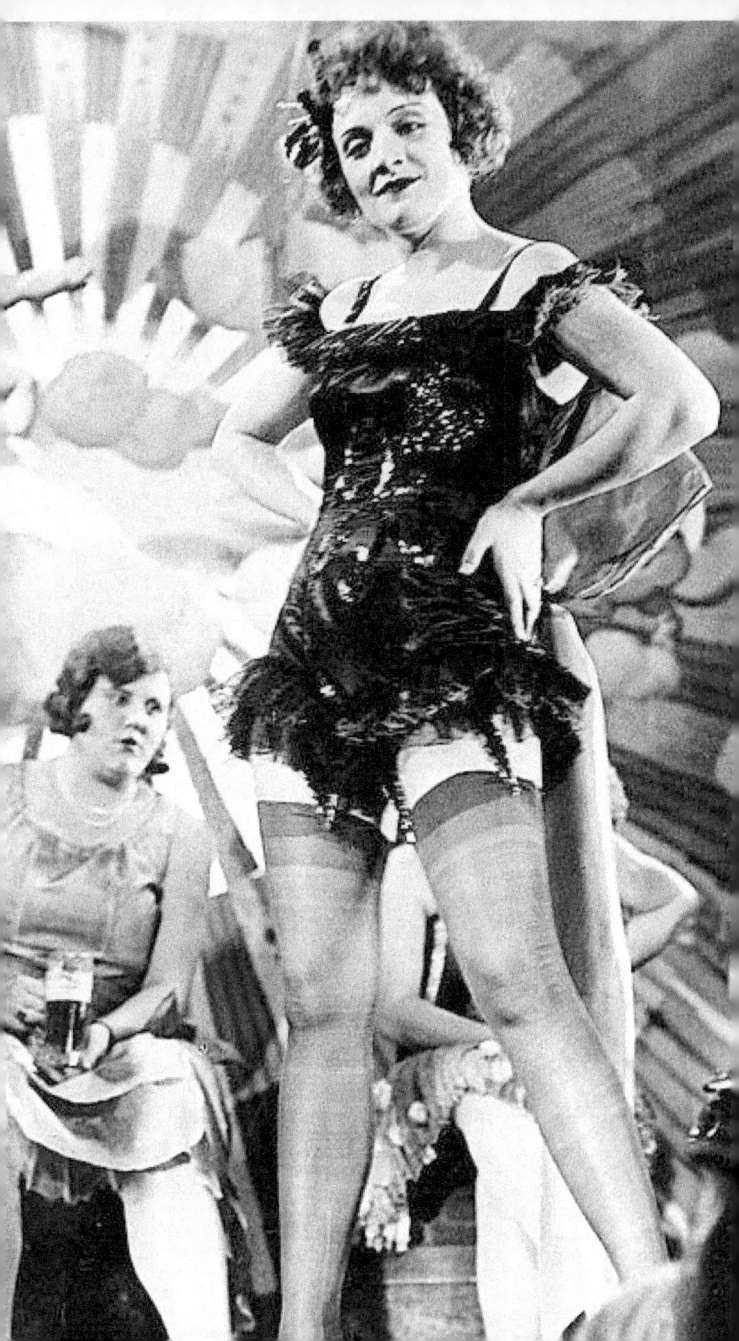

A lesser actress, perhaps someone trying too hard and pushing for sensuality on a more conventional scale, would have transformed Lola-Lola into a tyrant, a mean hearted she-devil using a love sick man as a toy, something to merely amuse her when she should fancy. But Dietrich handles it perfectly, torn between a flattery and genuine fondness and a carelessness which is impossible to avoid given the huge age difference and the way Jannings willingly degrades himself for her love. Though a guided performance led by the more experienced von Sternberg, Dietrich's naivety works in her favour. Some critics at the time claimed her acting skill to be so-so, but the flatness she harbours here makes the performance a successful one.

Another important point to make is that The Blue Angel, despite its sound, dialogue, music and legendary songs, is very much in its spirit a silent picture, though this may sound like a ludicrous contradiction when taken literally. The performances however have the purity of the best of silent film, when more is said in actions, especially the more subtle ones, than many of the actual lines. And Marlene handles herself as she had in her silent pictures, effortlessly gliding along, getting by on careful mannerisms and body language, suggestive behaviour and gestures. It's a tour de force of primal film performance, enhanced by the visual presentation rather than dialogue.

The visuals are all von Sternberg's, but the man himself admitted how much he relied on and needed Dietrich not just as a physical embodiment of his masochistic lusts, but as a collaborator with her own valid ideas. "I never had a better assistant than Miss Dietrich," he said as an older man, "if I wanted to sit down she brought me the chair. She did everything she could to understand me. She was very easy."

Dietrich herself recalled the collaboration on The Blue Angel with simplicity, suggesting that the analysis and theories about their masochistic relationship has perhaps been exaggerated down the years. "He just told me what I should do," she recalled later. "All directors do that but he was the very first director I had, so naturally I did exactly what he wanted."

Watching the film now, so aware of Dietrich's star power and strong persona in other films, The Blue Angel is an interesting document in regards to her development and moulding in the hands of her mentor. Clearly un-established, fresh faced and a little more filled out than the Dietrich of subsequent films, the roots of the icon are being planted and it is von Sternberg doing the watering. He saw in Marlene the very thing he was looking for, something that neither she nor the film studio could see for themselves. He was prophetic, but he was also vitally instrumental in ensuring that Dietrich fulfilling her potential.

The Blue Angel did set Marlene on the right path, but she was never that kind about it in her older years. She found Lola-Lola to be coarse, often diminished the film's reputation as an important landmark in cinema history and even said it was "enough to make you puke." One can understand why she would look down on her Hollywood debut, especially when you consider the more careful and calculated Dietrich of Shanghai Express and Morocco. In the later von Sternberg films and beyond, Marlene, though still guided by her directors, seems like a creation of her own, owned by herself and nobody else. She is powerful, assured and confident, whether embodying exoticism with effortless ease in Shanghai Express or fleeing conventions in her restless fugitive lifestyle in Blonde Venus. Here though, there is a virginal quality and it is evident that she is merely reflecting back the fantasies and masochistic perversions of von Sternberg.

Speaking in 1960 to The Observer, she made a reference to her image, the present one as an icon approaching sixty, and the one in the primitive Blue

Angel, clearly seeing a distinction between the two. "The image? A conglomerate of all the parts I've ever played on the screen. When I was in The Blue Angel people thought that was me: they really thought that was me!"

Even now, almost ninety years after it was made, the film has a stark brutality to it, an emotionally cold bluntness which has not dimmed down the decades. It's as if we are to delight in Janning/Rath's suffering, revel in the perversity of his breakdown. The Los Angeles Times wrote in 1991 that "it *is* often hard to stomach. Rath, a vulnerable but pedantic high school teacher, sinks way beyond his own protective self-righteousness after he encounters Lola-Lola. She's as immune to self-criticism as he is ruled by it. Lola-Lola is all impulse and sensuality; she's a sexual fantasy made real. This film can make you feel voyeuristic, especially by the queasy ending when Rath's ruin is complete. The famous rooster-crowing scene near the finale puts a man-gone-mad on display. The moment is emotionally over-inflated, but effective nonetheless."

There is a pointed, direct quality to The Blue Angel which was missing from the Dietrich/von Sternberg movies from here on. Marlene herself transformed too, from the knife voiced Lola-Lola to the more seductive, purring siren of Morocco and onwards, a slinkier and more graceful creature, more conscious too and well aware where the best lighting came from. But there is a freshness about Marlene in The Blue Angel which makes it exciting. Like watching Charlie Chaplin falling about in his early Keystone films, The Blue Angel gives the viewer an insight into the makings of a legend.

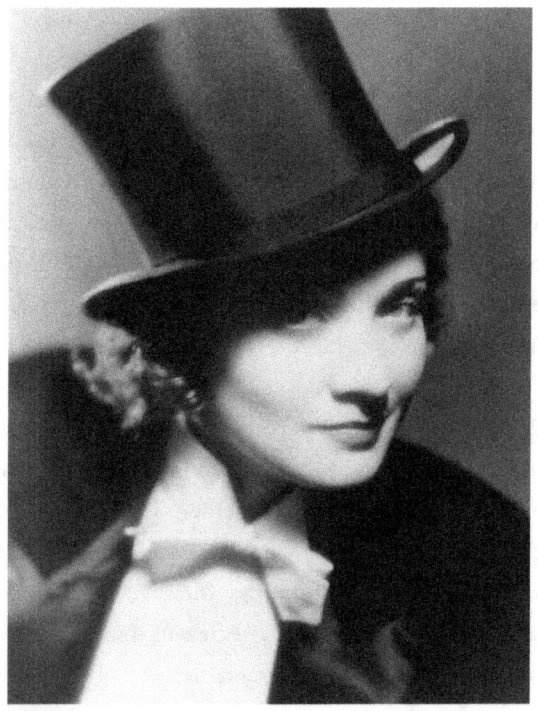

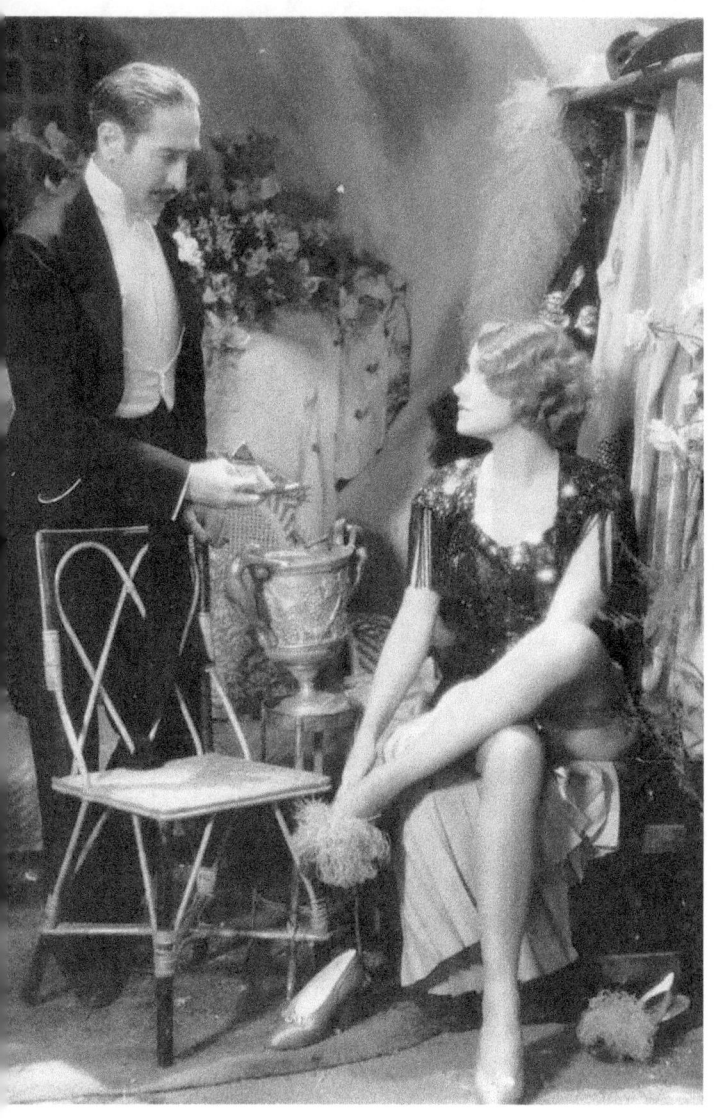

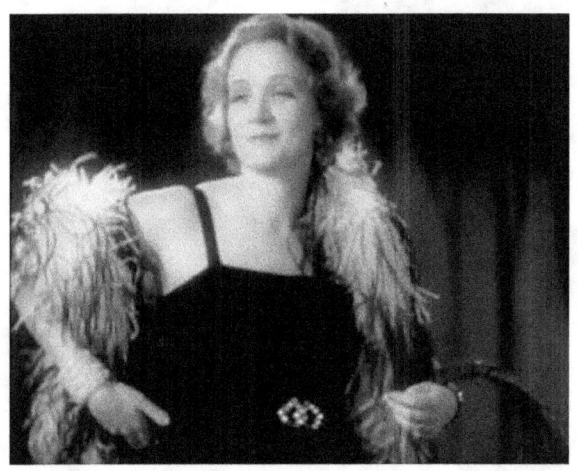

If The Blue Angel planted the roots of the legendary Dietrich, then Morocco was when the myth began to grow and bloom into something quite wonderful. Morocco itself was already in fruition before The Blue Angel was even released, and Paramount Pictures were well aware, prophetically at least, that Marlene was hot property and destined for stardom. Sternberg left Germany before the premiere of The Blue Angel for the bright lights of Hollywood, and Dietrich herself soon followed, after studio boss B.P. Schulberg was impressed by Marlene's Lola-Lola test footage. The image of Dietrich heading for movie land, leaving her daughter behind with a cargo of luggage, has entered movie history myth, and remains a vital part of the

Marlene story and her rise to success. She was thrust into the spotlight, raved up in the press as the hottest new star of the day, a new Garbo in fact, an import destined for stardom. Remarkably, Dietrich was hyped up as a star before The Blue Angel was even released, and she was accepted by the public with no questions asked. By the time Morocco appeared, fans were already flocking to see her in the theatres; by the time they left, they knew they would never forget the name of Marlene Dietrich.

In Morocco, Dietrich plays nightclub singer Amy Jolly, one of the passengers on a ship heading to Morocco, along with La Bessiere (Adolphe Menjou) who shows interest in Jolly. We are introduced to Tom Brown (Gary Cooper), a private in the army who enjoys Jolly's provocative stage act. Appearing in top hat and tails, Dietrich performs When Love Dies, kisses a woman on the lips and hands over her key to Tom, who later visits her house where they strike up a fondness for one another. Unbeknownst to him, he is being observed by the husband of his former lover, who just happens to be Tom's commanding officer, Caesar. He and Jolly are set about in the street by two thugs hired by Caesar, but Tom wins the fight. What follows is an old fashioned, at times hopelessly corny love story, with Tom almost losing Jolly to the rich La Besseriere.

Like all of Dietrich's finest films, the lasting impression of Morocco is in the moments, the iconic stand outs rather than the whole film itself. Though it has a plot that we are seriously invested in - even if we are aware it's all rather silly in a charming way - it is Dietrich who remains the reason we stick around. It isn't just Dietrich herself that we are glued to however, it is the very idea of Dietrich and the way she is presented to us. It's as if von Sternberg is unveiling some great work of art, a creation he is proud of and wants to show the world. She was arresting enough in The Blue Angel, but already in Morocco - a short span of time since her debut - the familiar, iconic Marlene of film legend has arrived. She has that look about her, slender, with almost pointed cheek bones and sharp features, the face that could stop traffic and eyes that say more with a glance than a whole page of dialogue. It's not so much about acting but owning the screen. From her opening number, Dietrich is charisma personified, not as giddy and naively playful was she was as Lola-Lola, but more sophisticated, therefore more irresistible. Her performance in top hat and tails may be overly familiar to many film buffs, but the decades since its release have not dimmed the magic of that sequence. It is sexy, subversive and beautifully performed, certainly one of the most important moments of pop culture from the whole of the 20th Century.

Though Dietrich's films often drip with innuendo, one notices the power of suggestion in Morocco beneath the surface, a much more subtle film than The Blue Angel. Cooper and Dietrich's romance is at the centre of the film, but they do not even speak to one another until some way into the film, making the whole thing a tease. But this works in the movie's favour, for just as Cooper feels the tension in Dietrich's seductive act and persona, so do us the viewers, putting us right beside the romantic lead in viewing Marlene as a seemingly unobtainable goddess.

Of course, all the credit cannot go to Dietrich, as appealing and magnetic as she may be. Undoubtedly the film would be much less without the visual imagination of Josef von Sternberg, and the lighting he perfected for Dietrich's angular features with the aid of Lee Garmes, the cinematographer. Sternberg once made a statement which summed up his whole career: "I care nothing about the story, only how it is photographed and presented. Shadow is mystery and light is clarity. Shadow conceals - light reveals. To know what to reveal and what to conceal and in what degrees to do this is all there is to art." Indeed, this could be his mantra, for in his movies with Dietrich the stories are often so oddly structured, ever winding and often erratic that they become secondary to the visuals. In fact, quite often, the more ludicrous they become (think the developments in the later Dishonoured for example) the more enjoyable the films become simply because the images are more striking. Quite often in a Dietrich/Sternberg movie you will come across a visual so arresting it could be framed and hung on a wall. Sternberg clearly thought in these terms, not as a storyteller but a visual stylist. If he was a slave to the image alone, than part of that image was Dietrich, a woman so liberated by her free sexuality, yet paradoxically also handcuffed to Sternberg's obsessive dreams.

From here on, Sternberg and Garmes to a lesser extent knew how to capture the best of Dietrich. It was all about the angle of the light, illuminating her correctly so the viewer would immediately know the emphasis was on her over the rest of the cast. She is elevated, existing somewhere above the often inconsequential plot and in a realm of her own. It's in the shadows, the power of Dietrich through the lens of von Sternberg, as she slinks her way through the exotic, high camp surroundings. Even until the very end, with Dietrich on the Moroccan sand in quest for her true love, von Sternberg is clear who our attention should be on, and just who out of the many actors in the film should live longest in our memories after the movie is over.

Today, Morocco, like many of Dietrich and von Sternberg's other films, is more known for the iconography than the story or film harbouring the legendary Dietrich stand outs. Images of her in the top hat have become so iconic that most people take the innovative qualities of Dietrich's part in the film for granted. But movie history is made up of single scenes and even single frames, moments which refuse to leave the public's consciousness despite the march of time. Dietrich's very appearance in Morocco, and even the publicity stills which show off her suggestive smirk with cigarette in hand, are enough to ensure that if not the film then at least Dietrich's Amy Jolly is firmly imbedded into film legend. In a way it almost doesn't matter that most people will pass on seeking out a film like Morocco and be more satisfied with the image and idea of Dietrich, the romanticised still preserved in sepia, than the walking, talking, moving Dietrich on celluloid. At least in this way her legend lives on healthily, if only superficially.

Film scholars and academics have often written of the biblical subtext in Morocco, a thin concept it must be said, mostly borne out of the scene when Dietrich is handing out apples after her performance and the jokes in song which apparently allude to an Adam and Eve symbolism beneath the surface. But I don't feel one needs to perform such an academic study of a film like Morocco, which is purely a stylistic slice of escapism, especially if one comes out with a theory which would have made Dietrich roll her eyes impatiently. What matters is the film, but more so the images, those preserved visuals, with von Sternberg as painter of masterpieces and Dietrich as his muse.

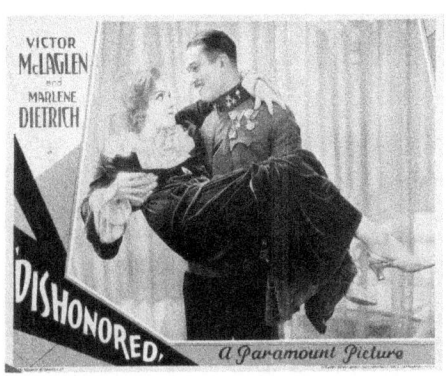

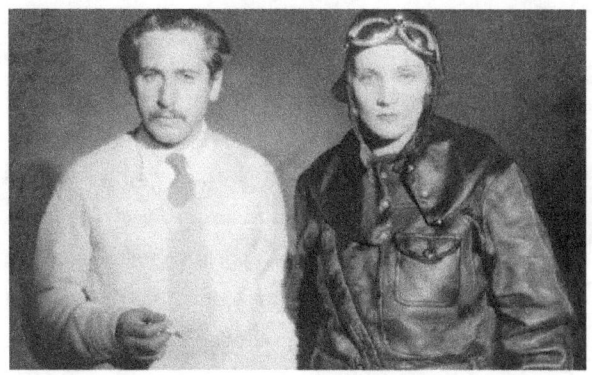

Dishonoured, though in some ways perhaps the most interesting collaboration between Dietrich and von Sternberg, is probably the least celebrated and talked about of their seven films, with he as visionary and she as idolised icon. Coming after The Blue Angel and Morocco, both of which established Dietrich as the ultimate object of desire, Dishonoured takes her glamorous persona a stage further and turns her into a myth. It is here that Dietrich the great untouchable being comes into her own.

The film itself begins beautifully, illustrating von Sternberg's knack of capturing stark visuals, here of the harsh, rainy, unforgiving city, with heavy dissolves and imaginative camera movements. We zone in on Vienna, during the war in 1915, one rainy night in particular as a body is being taken out of a block of flats in the red light district of the city. As the crowd gathers, it is clear the corpse is a prostitute who has taken her own life. Enter Dietrich, a fellow night prowler who declares "I am not afraid of life, although I am not afraid of death either." Our first sight of Dietrich is, of course, her legs (*those* legs I should add), and immediately she is a figure of great mystery and appeal. As she flees the scene and heads back to her lodgings, she is followed by the Chief of the Secret Service (Gustav von Seyfferitz), intrigued by her poetic view of existence. He sees potential in Dietrich, and seeing as he has been searching for an attractive woman to sign up as a spy, sees her as an ideal candidate. With the chief masquerading as a foreign agent to test her loyalty for her country, she alerts the police who then take him away, convincing the chief that as she stayed loyal, as he suspected, she will make a great spy.

Dietrich is known as Frau, a war widow with an apartment full of interesting knick knacks, a beloved black cat and a piano, which she plays brutally in the first apartment scene. The piano will return to the plot later as Frau illustrates her skill on the instrument. When she is summoned to the main headquarters of the Secret Service, the chief gives her the spy code name of X 27, and sets her to work. Her opening mission is to reveal two spies at a masked ball, a great sequence bordering on the purely surreal, in which Dietrich succeeds with flying colours. She ends up on the Polish border to sneak out Russian military plans, but her methods are criticised by Captain Kranau (Victor McLagen) who disapproves of her using sexuality and her feminine graces to achieve her goals.

In a sequence which illustrates Dietrich's under-valued acting range, she poses as a peasant girl in Russia working as a chambermaid, with her loyal feline by her side of course. The plot thickens, as a musical score acts as a secret code. Eventually, in an unexpected turn, X 27 is convicted of treason and sentenced to death. Though we presume the young soldier who has a soft spot for her may reverse the decision, he does not have such power, and the execution is acted out brutally and without empathy, sending Dietrich, riddled with bullets (though with no signs of blood thankfully), flying to the ground like a broken marionette.

When it came to plot, most of von Sternberg and Dietrich's films were ridiculous, though it was the kind of ridiculous we tend to enjoy. In fact, the more ludicrous the story line got, the more potential there was for von Sternberg to place his elegant muse in all manner of scenarios and settings. Dishonoured, with its far out story that though meandering at times delivers a fatal final punch that blows away all the preceding convolution, offers Dietrich so much as an actress but more importantly as a star. It's a showcase for her as a movie idol yes, but it also shows off her more varied abilities as a visual centre piece, the kind of which cinema history has chosen to sideline in favour of the spoilt rich glamour goddess image. She is not degraded as an object but elevated as a wonder. This is an important distinction.

It is clear from their third film together that von Sternberg is not so much in love with his star, but obsessed with her. Unable to own and possess her in real life, he perversely tortures himself in the films by elevating her ever higher, ensuring she is unobtainable. There is a masochistic tendency here, though von Sternberg would never have admitted the fact he worshipped Dietrich. Instead he put in older characters who acted as von Sternberg doppelganger cuckolds, men who knew that Dietrich was out of their grasp. His obsession with Marlene though, often overshadows anything that happens in the film around or behind her, and from beginning to end it is she who remains our focal point.

The vision and style may be von Sternberg's, but the film really belongs to Dietrich herself. She admitted that von Sternberg was the man who made her and without him she would never have become the Dietrich we all know and love, but there is undoubtedly a natural glow around her that movie lights and sets, not to mention costumes and hair styles, only enhance. In every scene she is set up to stun the viewer, to grab the attention, and indeed, even when doing a little tired stretch in her apartment, hinting to the Chief that it's time for him to go, she oozes sex appeal. But there is also humour present, suggesting that Dietrich is not taking herself entirely seriously. There is an added comedic value to the piano scenes, especially when a frantic Dietrich is hammering away at the tune, then turning swiftly to the sheer amazement at the group of men gathered round her, helpless as animals, as she decodes the message. The word camp is thrown around a lot these days, and in the way Christopher Isherwood meant it, Dietrich and von Sternberg's Dishonoured is high camp. The masked ball scene, the maid sequence and in particular the striking execution, are all heavily stylised yet retain their individual power. Ludicrous yes, but never laughable.

There is also the fact that, like The Blue Angel, Dietrich is a vision of female empowerment, just as she was, admittedly in more varied ways, in future collaborations with von Sternberg. In Shanghai Express she reduces all men to dribbling wrecks with her sexuality; in Blonde Venus she was frowned upon for abandoning the supposed rigidity of motherhood and family life, but came out a revolutionary female all the same; here she proves that as a spy she can more than match the men, even if her grisly fate suggests she will never be truly equal in the eyes of the system. Again though, Dietrich doesn't need a man, even if society tells her she does. As X 27 she is strong, powerful in fact, self assured and confident in a male dominated world. Though she is unfairly put to death, she does not shed a tear or show a hint of fear as the guns raise towards her. Until her dying moment she retains her dignity, yet the subsequent coldness felt by the males who took her life, leaving the room while the bullets still echo, is so unsettling that it makes one wonder if her struggle was worth it.

Plot and film so often became secondary to the star in Hollywood's Golden era, but here it seems more than ever the film exists mostly for its glamorous star. That said, Dietrich's glow robs nothing from the director, and von Sternberg uses every opportunity to show off his skills, to linger on visuals few other directors of the time, especially American filmmakers, would even dream of. Yes, focus is mostly on Dietrich's magical prowess, but she is aided by fascinating surroundings, captured beautifully by a von Sternberg in full control.

In 1968 von Sternberg wrote that he directed actors "by producing perhaps a trance, a sort of mesmerism otherwise unknown, by blotting out their traits and substituting a behaviour alien to them, by gesture and mimicry, by the drama of light and shade, by foiling every obstruction, by movement and angle of the camera, by constant alertness to voice and cadence, and most important of all—by inspecting oneself."

This trance is evident in other Dietrich collaborations, mostly Shanghai Express, but it's present in Dishonoured too. There is no need for background music, or extravagant indulgences that Hollywood's hired men would have employed. Josef lends the film an unreal quality, with actors as machines almost, creating a film which is hypnotic, soothing even, otherworldly at times. Dietrich, with her strange, individual voice and quirky way of delivering the English dialogue, lends herself to the dream-like world wonderfully, giving the feeling one is in a state of beautiful, heavenly delirium.

The film was rushed into production by Paramount after the high smash success of The Blue Angel and Morocco, based on the story of the infamous Dutch spy Mata Hari. Josef himself objected to the title which was chosen, insisting that X 27 was never dishonoured as the posters suggested. Though he felt this betrayed his vision of Dietrich, the female among the alpha males who died with honour rather than dishonour, von Sternberg did not have the power to override Paramount's decisions. Ever one to compete, MGM panicked at the sight of Dietrich as the Hari-esque spy and speedily put together a project starring her "rival", Greta Garbo, more successful at the box office but today much more dated.

Considering the many joys of Dishonoured, especially for fans of simply basking in Dietrich's beauty, Dishonoured is still one of the least appreciated of her collaborations with von Sternberg. When it is mentioned in David A Cook's A History of Narrative Film, it gets a quick summarisation as "sardonic and not particularly inspired", which seems misinformed.

If the film hasn't endured as one of her widely loved movies, it was nicely received in some quarters in the day, at least by those who understood Dietrich's appeal. In Richard Watts' review he wrote "of Miss Dietrich, it need only be said that she proves once more that her hasty ride to film celebrity was the result of neither luck or publicity. There still may be some doubt whether she possesses that technical expertness on which so many observers place such store, but there can be little question by now that her almost lyrically ironic air of detachment and, to be frank, her physical appeal, make her one of the great personages of the local drama."

In his book on Dietrich, Homer Dickens wrote that the role was "perfectly suited to the Dietrich face, manner, voice and style. This offered more acting range than Dietrich had thus far known under von Sternberg. She was not only creating varying moods, but was letting herself be created within those moods. Thus we see many Dietrichs in the film."

While it may have its admirers, Dishonoured is one of those Dietrich gems drifting more and more into obscurity, into the dusty vaults so to speak. But has its fans it certainly does. This intoxicating spell of a film remains as bewitching now as no doubt it was back in 1931.

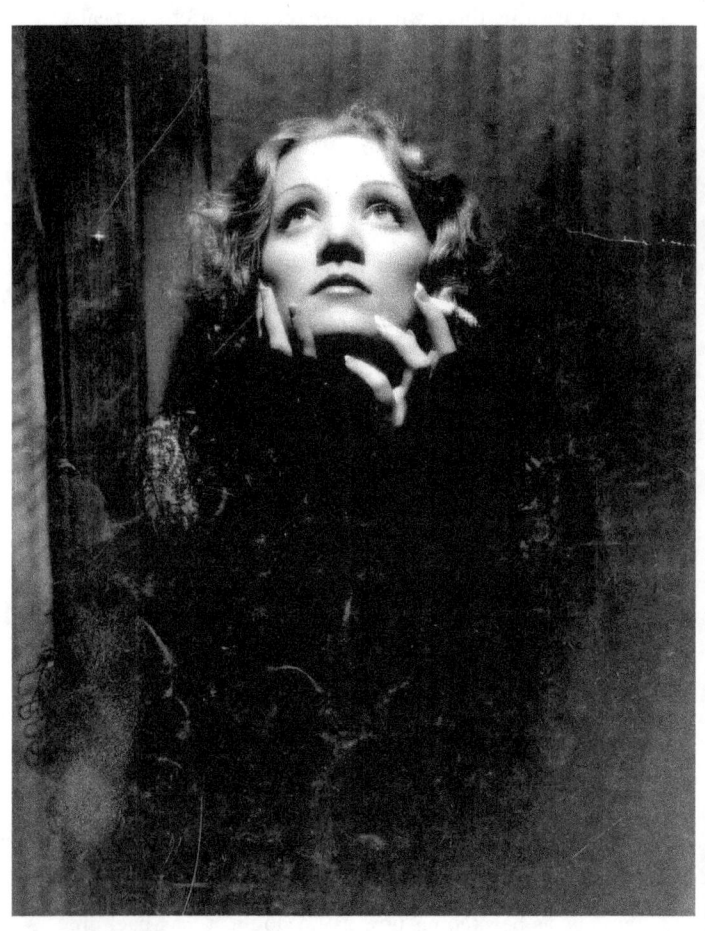

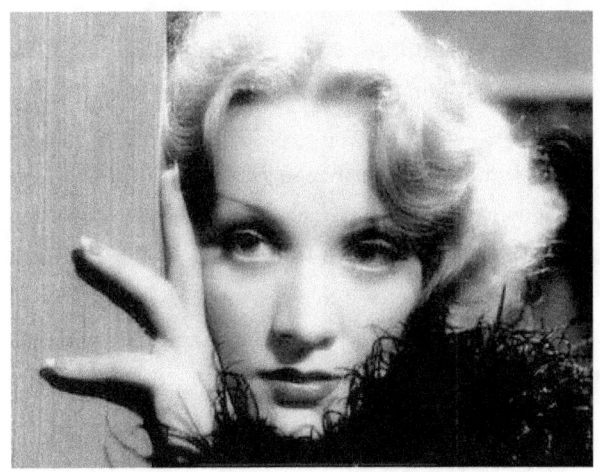

Shanghai Express is widely considered to be the pinnacle of Dietrich and von Sternberg's collaborations. Some of the other films they made together may be superior in other areas, yet in regards to presenting as Dietrich as perfect idol, a glamour icon completely out of reach to us mere mortals, Shanghai Express has no competition. It was also the biggest commercial success of the Dietrich and von Sternberg pictures, making nearly 4 million at the time in the US alone; clearly, an America suffering during the Great Depression found Dietrich and her immortal beauty a most satisfying distraction.

Shanghai Express is based on the story by Henry Harvey, concerning a train heading from Peking to Shanghai during the Chinese Civil War in 1931. Clive

Brook plays British Captain Donald Harvey, whose friends tell him he will be sharing the train with the famous Shanghai Lily, played by Dietrich, who actually turns out to be a former lover named Madeline, with whom he enjoyed a passionate affair before she was known around the world under her new pseudonym. Their affair had ended five years earlier when a ploy set up by Lily resulted in him leaving her, but as is clear from their first meeting together, there are still feelings between the pair.

We are also introduced to other passengers on the express train, such as Lily's friend Hui Fei, played by the terrific Anna May Wong, eccentric English woman Mrs Haggerty (Louise Closser Hale in a dotty performance) and the strange, mistrustful Henry Chang, who is portrayed by Warner Oland.

A plot soon develops when the Chinese Government come on board in search of a rebel leader, and later on, thanks to Chang who sends a message out, the train is taken over by the rebel army, the leader of whom is Chang himself, who suddenly turns out to be a much more sinister character than we first thought. Chang discovers that Captain Harvey is on his way to perform surgery on the Governor General of Shanghai, so needs him alive. Meanwhile Chang has his eyes on making

Shanghai Lily his mistress, who uses his infatuation with her in a secret scheme to free the express train from the vicious rebels.

Oddly, when written out, the plot seems more exciting and engaging than it actually is on screen. The way von Sternberg paces the film and its thin storyline is rather unusual, in that the dialogue itself and the way it is delivered is flat, almost robotic in fact. The truth is that von Sternberg encouraged this mechanical way of speaking to emulate the rhythms of the train. It may make for a slightly odd, disjointed viewing, but the voices and mannerisms do indeed blend in with the chugging grind of the engine. Acted in this way, the plot never feels sensational or unbelievable. Yes the film has a strangely surreal air to it, thanks to the performances, but there is no dramatic music, no flamboyant camera movements to enhance any of the action, and there is never a sense of phony heightened excitement. Indeed, Shanghai Express is as steady and immovable as the grind of the train the characters are on board.

Paramount Pictures knew that a von Sternberg and Dietrich picture would always be costly, because costumes, lighting and sets had to look a certain way and von Sternberg himself insisted on taking his time to achieve what he had set out to. They weren't always guaranteed hits of course (some of their other movies had been disappointments at the box office) but Paramount seemed happy enough to let the director indulge himself, as well as his most vivid fantasies. And let's face it, von Sternberg's most vivid fantasy, his wildest infatuation, his true obsession, was Marlene Dietrich herself.

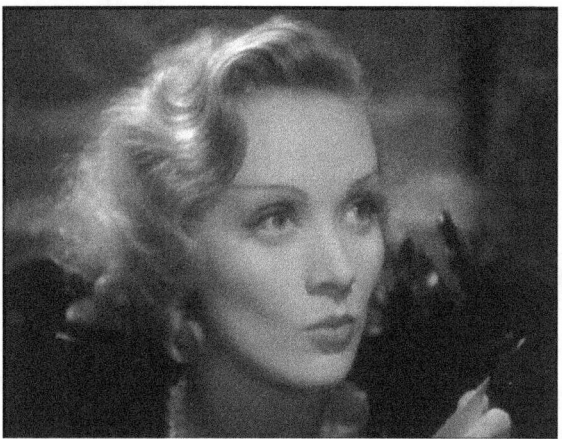

This brings us to what is at the epicentre of this whole exercise in style and mood, Marlene, his goddess of glamour, whose very presence dominates the film. Everything that happens, every word, every line, every scene, every costume, every lavish set, and every set up is to lend gravitas to the arrival of Dietrich. When she's not on camera the viewer is thinking about when she will appear next, and when she's being filmed in all her glory we cannot take our eyes off her. If von Sternberg's aim was to make a fetishistic item out of not just Dietrich herself but the very idea of her, then he succeeded.

Not so much as acting but more just "being" in the purest sense, Marlene is the embodiment of old style movie star charisma. Her exotic looks dazzle, her costumes hang on to her slender frame and her lines, often purred seductively, often spoken in that classic disjointed Dietrich manner, come forth like mini quotable nuggets, not realistic in any way, but highly memorable for that fact alone. When she isn't speaking, Dietrich is a walking - or still-standing - work of art for the ever hungry von Sternberg, who seemed to get a thrill out of placing her in increasingly bizarre circumstances and positions. Shanghai Express is a film yes, one with a plot that while easy to follow is still properly worked out, but for the most part this is movie not just as moving painting, but as showcase for Dietrich.

It's worth noting that critics and admirers say it was Shanghai Express that made her a glamour icon and firm household name, and it's fair to say that it wasn't the film itself that enhanced her popularity but her appearance, or even more specifically, her presentation, unveiled as she is like a great timeless masterpiece, within the picture itself. This was the fourth time von Sternberg and Dietrich had worked together, and by now he was an expert in Dietrich lighting. With Dietrich it was all about shadows, the spaces, where to place lights to accentuate her looks, her lips, her cheekbones, and perhaps most vitally of all, her legs. It might be wrong to call Dietrich's work in Shanghai Express a performance, for it is more of a reveal, an act of showmanship, a magic act in some regards, and a master class in effortlessly stealing scenes by just being present. Yes she was aided by a director who knew his star's best angles, and a brilliant cinematographer, Lee Games, who won an Academy Award for the film (Marlene later gave most of the credit to von Sternberg himself, who obviously guided the cinematography), but Dietrich's self control and knowledge of her own power were vital factors in this glamour tour de force. The impact is also aided by tension. Dietrich's first appearance in the film is through a veil which covers half her face. As if to tease and titillate the viewer, von Sternberg does not reveal the enigmatic Dietrich until she is on board. Before then she is spoken of with excitement, a mythical character in her own life time. Once we are on board the train, Lily becomes the focal point for our senses; the plot is secondary, and the other cast members standing by for the arrival of Dietrich's quietly towering presence. She does not need to try hard; she is effortlessly a star in every way.

Reviewers were impressed by the film upon its release, but most of all by Dietrich's star power. Many noted the control she had over her part and the audience. The New York Times praised her, writing, "Miss Dietrich gives an impressive performance. She is languorous but fearless as Lily. She glides through her scenes with heavy eyelids and puffing on her cigarettes. She measures every word and yet she is not too slow in her foreign-accented speech. Brooks' performance is also noteworthy, but he speaks in a monotone and is a little too hasty sometimes in his replies in conversations with Miss Dietrich."

Shanghai Express succeeds because it does not try to convince the viewer it is not a motion picture. This is escapism pure and simple, beautifully lit and photographed in seductive black and white, tasteful and assured in every scene, with all emphasis on the appeal of Dietrich. Josef von Sternberg became well known for his slow dissolves, which though began to tire some people a few pictures in, are handled masterfully here. The way the sequences blend together makes the transitions natural, often seamless, compared to the often jarring quality of some early sound pictures. And though one can fairly say that the delivery of the dialogue may put off modern viewers (there is, after all, almost a complete lack of emotion in the film), anyone with the patience to enjoy this film for what it is will be convinced that the technique works brilliantly. If anything, the disjointed speaking enhances the fact that we are in von Sternberg's alternative world, a place where myth and reality blend together to create a kind of enhanced dream state, emotionally stunted yet stylistically controlled.

Modern viewers attuned to fast moving plots, breakneck paces and snappily delivered dialogue may find Shanghai Express painfully old fashioned and slow. For others however, the film will come across as a soothing escape from modernity, a film which though fairly short feels endless in the best possible way. To compliment the film further, I would say that as soon as it finishes it would not be an odd choice to put it back on again, or to even having it showing in the background as you go about your day. There is a quality here that makes the movie a comforting pleasure, a treat. Shanghai Express is a classy, surrealistic distraction which may tread carefully through its flimsy plot, but does so with such grace that one wouldn't object to it being three hours long. The people and the words they speak blend wonderfully in with the visuals, as if being sucked into the hypnotism of the whole piece. We are in von Sternberg's fantasy now, and Dietrich is the queen of this hazy indulgence.

Though von Sternberg had made other great films together, and would do so again the same year with Blonde Venus, there is a quality to Shanghai Express which makes it so otherworldly, so unique in is flatness, which ensures it will remain their seminal collaboration. While other early talkies from the age seem jerky and irrelevant, Shanghai Express is timeless, a film for all the ages; and it is also vintage Dietrich, sure proof that she was perhaps the most appealing and watchable of all the classic female stars of the Golden era.

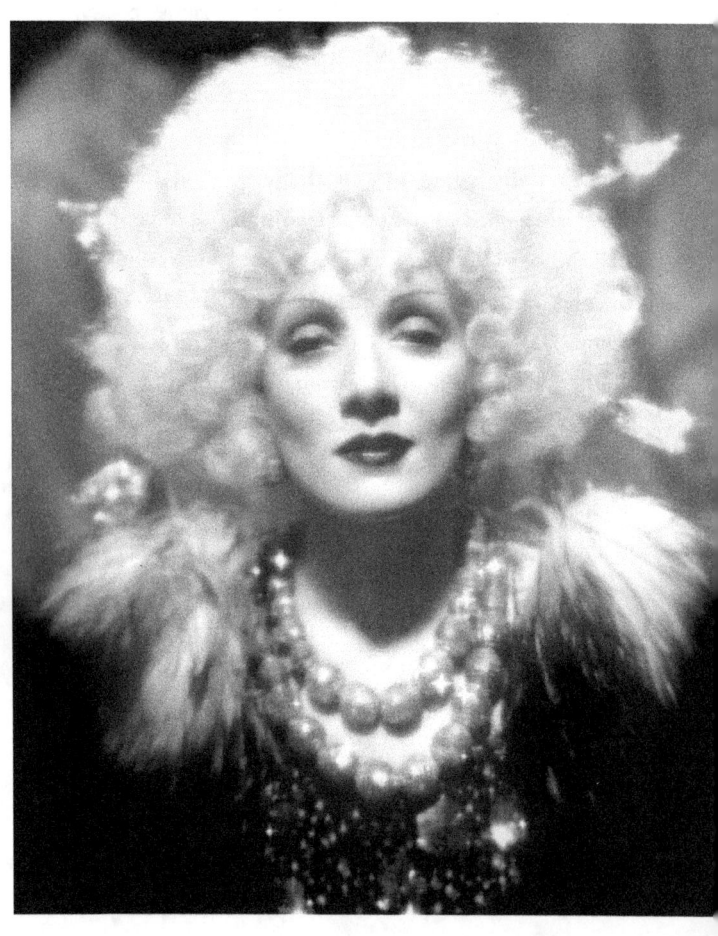

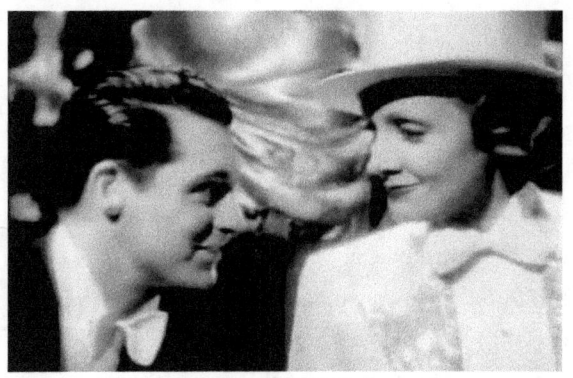

Blonde Venus marked a big change in Marlene Dietrich's on screen career. Granted, she was still centre stage as she had been in the previous four von Sternberg movies, but here her character moved further away from being von Sternberg's fetishist icon and towards a more proto-feministic direction. Blonde Venus, released the same year as Shanghai Express, still placed Dietrich as a figure of extreme glamour, but it also depicted her as a woman, a multi faceted character, and perhaps most importantly, a mother.

In the build up to her arrival in Hollywood and elevation to world stardom, Paramount's film publicity cunningly ensured that potential fans were reminded frequently that Dietrich was a family woman. She was depicted in interviews as being a devoted mother, and time and time again was photographed alongside her daughter Maria. Things were not as perfect as they seemed to be in reality, but the truth was that the public, one increasingly aware of Dietrich as a superstar and icon of beauty, loved the motherly side of Marlene. It's a surprise then that Paramount waited until her fifth Hollywood picture to properly depict her as a mother. In Blonde Venus she plays one role, but it's a well rounded one, not merely a caricature of idealised perfection and womanhood. She's a dancer yes, but she's also a loving wife, and a committed mother. This was a more three-dimensional Dietrich, slightly nudged if not removed from her pedestal. But was this a Dietrich the world was ready to accept?

Blonde Venus begins beautifully with a breathtaking sequence depicting Dietrich as some exotic water nymph, and again, von Sternberg has us at a distance gawping at her fabulousness. She is cavorting in a pond with five other girls, all naked, somewhere in Germany, watched over by seven American students. Helen (Marlene Dietrich), clearly the bluntest of the ladies, tells them all to clear off, though one man, Ned (played by Herbert Marshall) stubbornly refuses.

We then cut away, but water is a linking image. It is a few years later, and Dietrich, looking decidedly less glamorous, earthier perhaps, and in some ways more approachable (dare I say relatable?), is bathing a small boy in a bath. She and Ned ended up marrying and having a child, but their happy life together has been cut short by the news that Ned has been poisoned by radium and predicts he will be dead within a year. He visits a doctor who tells him that if he were willing to pay $1500 and travel across Germany he could meet a physician who may be able to cure him of this supposed death sentence.

Then there is a lovely scene of Ned and Helen putting their son to bed, with Marlene telling their son the story of how they met before singing a sweet song while winding up a music box as the boy drifts sweetly to sleep. Ned and Helen then discuss the matter of the expensive treatment, and Helen comes up with the idea of going back to the stage to raise the cash. Ned is hesitant if not outright objectionable to the idea, but in the end Helen goes along to a club to get theatre work as a performer. After performing her sensational and famous Hot Voodoo routine (where Dietrich comes on stage in an ape costume which she then removes) she meets Nick Townsend (Cary Grant), a rich politician who instantly has a thing for her. Though infatuated with Dietrich herself, he gives her $300 towards her husband's treatment.

Speedily, Dietrich has enough to pay the medical bills and though lying to her husband about where the money came from, she sends him off to the specialist. After she and her son see Ned off to sea, Nick arrives and gives her a lift home. He promises her free boarding at a friend's apartment, and won over by Nick's kindness, she begins to fall for him. Though she loves Ned, Helen agrees to go on vacation with Nick, just as Ned arrives home early from his treatment, where he finds his wife gone. Ned then discovers the truth of her quitting the stage and pairing up with Nick, promising to give her back every penny she earned for his treatment. When Ned says he will fight Helen for custody of their son, she fleas the house and goes on the run. She spends a large part of the film fleeing the police, and when she realises she is in too deep, that this restless fugitive existence is damaging for her son, she hands him over to Nick and goes on her way.

In a marvellous scene, Dietrich has a kind of breakdown where she throws all her money away by giving it to a down and out in a women's safe house. Though her prospects look bleak at this point, she picks herself up and hits the stage, where she ends up as a star in Paris. Reunited with Nick, she tells him how much she misses her son, and being a gentleman he is urged by his conscience to take her back home to America to be with her son. In a final scene, beautiful in its old fashioned purity and simplicity, a reunited Helen and Ned are putting their son to bed. Comforted by the sight of his parents together again, the boy asks to hear the tale of how they met. Helen winds up the same music box from the start of the film, which we see in a long close up which seems to reflect the merry go round journey we are all on in life, but especially Helen herself, who now realises home is where the heart is. Though she and Ned will not immediately return to how they once were, they both know that they belong with one another.

Blonde Venus takes Dietrich out of the stagey settings of her previous films and into the real world, all over a vast and dangerous America and then into a glamorous Paris. Her journey is an epic one of self discovery, an adventure into the world but also into herself. Despite all the travelling and performing, the promises of wealth from Nick and the life style he could have given her, she knows that simple little house, with Ned and her son by her side, is all that she needs. It may seem simplistic in the eyes of modern viewers, but the message is still valid and can be applied to life itself for all of us. The grass may look greener over yonder, but it's not so bad on this side either.

Strangely enough, it was this widening of the scope, turning Dietrich into a wild outlaw in the jungle of life, which prompted reviewers to cast their doubts on the Dietrich/Sternberg partnership. The New York Times for instance wrote that Blonde Venus was a "muddled, unimaginative and generally hapless piece of work, relieved somewhat by the talent and charm of the German actress..."

The film was written by von Sternberg with S.K. Lauren and Jules Furthman, and it needs to be added that in his autobiography von Sternberg himself said it was written "swiftly to provide something other than the sob stories that were being submitted." Josef knew his star well enough to be sure that standard Hollywood claptrap, the aforementioned sob stories, would do Dietrich no good, and that she had to be in control of her circumstances, no matter what the role. Vitally it seems, Helen is at times lost and very much in need, but she never reaches out for a man's guidance. She may take money from Nick, but ultimately she is her own woman; so much so in fact that in the last part of the picture she is liberated from the burden of her son and takes to life as a sole entity, where, importantly it seems, she succeeds. She is no longer bogged down by the temptations from Nick, the neediness of Ned and her son. The Blonde Venus arrives when Helen is free enough to welcome her.

All this of course may have been hard for audiences in 1932 to accept. After all, in the eyes of backward thinking men, women belonged at home, and any female expressing a desire to do anything away from the stove was hushed. On screen, women were usually fancy frills, eye candy or love interest for the dashing heroic males. Dietrich then was way ahead of her time, especially in her von Sternberg films. One needs to only look at that run of films - Dishonoured which saw her as a spy put to death, Shanghai Express which had her as the ultimate male fantasy and Blonde Venus as a trailblazing feminist rebelling from the family constraints - to see she was a cut above the other female leads of the day. Unlike other actresses, she did not cry out for our sympathy, or even for us to like her. What Dietrich did though, through her charisma, was force us to at least care, and in Blonde Venus, a film that is nearly ninety years old, we root for her in her ragtag journey towards inner peace and acceptance.

As an actual film, in visual terms, Blonde Venus is not quite as stylish and slick as Shanghai Express, but it certainly had more in terms of content that its predecessor, if not in style. Express, as great as it is, was more of a showcase for Dietrich's poses, her enigmatic appeal, her exotic radiance etc. Blonde Venus however showed her not just as a beautiful woman, but also as a mother, often unglamorous, and a very flawed woman. She was egocentric and ruthless, but in the end, for all her shortcomings, a decent human being at heart. The previous von Sternberg films lacked this depth. What Blonde Venus often lacks in frilliness it makes up for with story, its sense of exhausted desperation when she's on the run, and the more complex performance from Dietrich. On top of that of course are the wonderful stage routines, with Dietrich excelling in the Hot Voodoo number and sizzling in her white top hat and tails sequence.

Cinematographer Bert Glennon does a great job with the film, making Dietrich look great even when in her ordinary, every day domestic setting. Dietrich may be seen as this unapproachable woman to whom household chores are a mystery, but she also pulls off her scenes as the doting mother and homemaker. At the same time, she still looks worthy of movie star idolisation, again this partly down to the photography.

On the other end of things, the song sequences are also photographed wonderfully well. At this stage, the world's image of Dietrich was already so firmly established that she looked like a true veteran in the stage sequences. This was down to her experience on the stage which went back over a decade, but it was also down to confidence; note her relaxed mood on the final song routine and you will see Dietrich is sure of herself and her immovable stardom. She must have known all too well that her name would now be forever known to the public.

Today, Blonde Venus is seen as one of the least notable of Marlene and Josef's collaborations, which seems unjustified when you consider what it has going for it; the songs are enough to ensure a legendary status, while the forward thinking slant on the free woman should if anything enhance its historical importance. Save for Hot Voodoo however, which often gets singled out as a career highlight (usually in reference to her innuendo laden songs) and the white tuxedo number (itself seen as a pale copy of the admittedly much sexier Morocco routine), Blonde Venus seems to have been largely ignored down the years. In the cult of Marlene however, it is a match for Shanghai Express and Morocco, illustrating the fact that Dietrich was much more than a pretty face well lit.

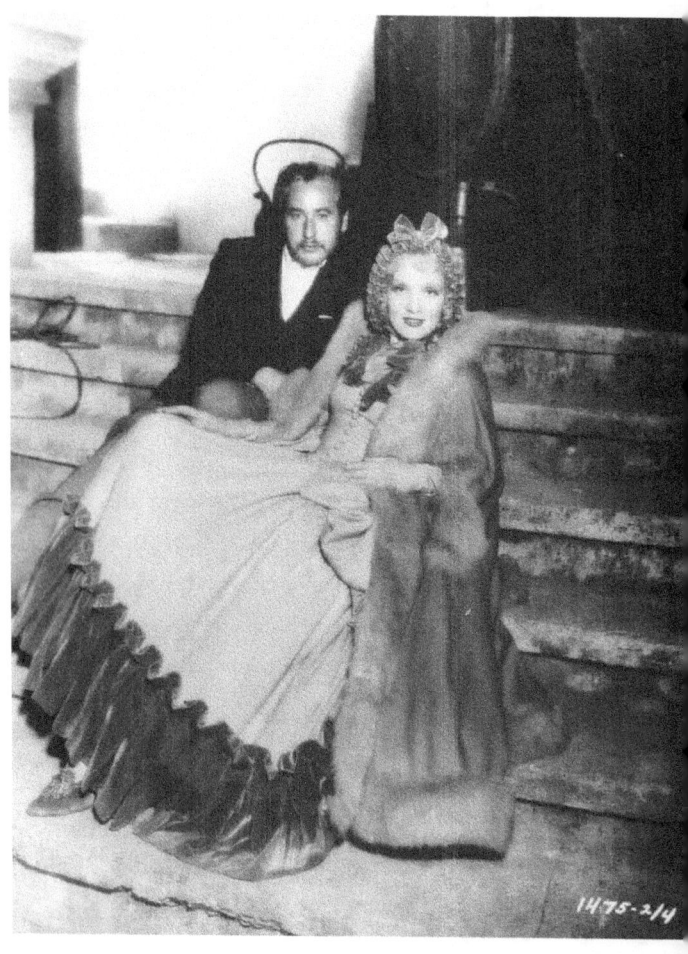

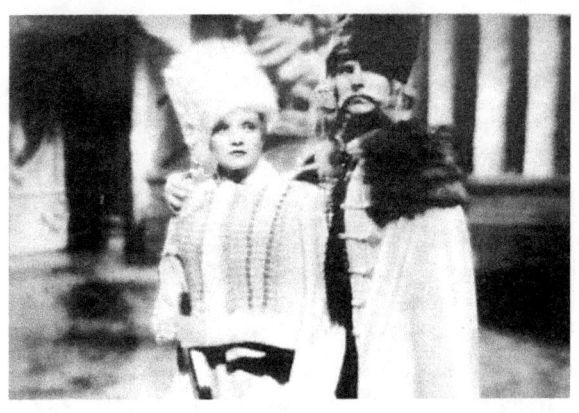

The last two films Marlene and Josef made together were The Scarlet Empress and The Devil is a Woman. The former, made in 1934 and featuring Dietrich as Catherine the Great, was according to von Sternberg himself, "a relentless excursion into style". Again though, this is not a case of pure style over content. Granted, the film does not pretend to be depicting the true story of Catherine the Great, and there is a level of camp here very high even for Marlene and Josef's collaborations, but there is a grace to both the film and Marlene's assured performance that fully elevates the exercise. Yes, the idea of a modern glamour figure such as Dietrich playing the powerful empress might understandably raise a titter or two, but Dietrich becomes the part, oozes pure class and embodies the hierarchal dignity of the great leader wonderfully.

At the time of release, The Scarlet Empress was often pitted against 1933's Queen Christina, featuring her so called rival Greta Garbo, but in reality von Sternberg's biopic has little in common with the earlier Garbo flick. For one, the direction is much tidier, the lighting accentuating Dietrich's wonderful features and creating a general moodiness not apparent in Queen Christina. Dietrich's performance was not a million miles from Garbo's however, and both used their European exoticism and love of suggestive sexuality to create convincing portrayals. But there really was no rivalry at all, both women clearly being above such childishness.

The Scarlet Empress charts the journey of Sophia (Dietrich), daughter of a German prince and a mother who aspires for a better life for her daughter. Sent to Russia, she marries the nephew of Empress Elizabeth to marry her nephew, Grand Duke Peter, but becomes bored, renaming herself Catherine and amusing herself with Count Alexey Razumovsky, a womaniser who it turns out is courting the Empress. Catherine aligns herself with the Russians and when Duke Peter finds himself in power after the demise of the Empress, Catherine takes no prisoners and pushes for a reign, redubbing herself as Catherine the Great, a woman who so famously rose to the top against all odds.

Of course, this being Dietrich and Von Sternberg, reality comes second to fantasy and presentation. Heavily stylised, Russia becomes a backward, stunted land on the cusp of collapse, over reliant on tradition and the kind of foreboding religious imagery not present in the real Russia of the day. Still, the gargoyle screams carved in rock make for good metaphor for a land in need of a drastic change, one no doubt to be brought in by Catherine the Great. Besides, such gothic imagery is naturally perfect fodder for von Sternberg, master of shadows, mystery and dissolve.

Dietrich herself is wonderful, dominating the film completely in a performance that is confident yet fuss free. She takes charge of the screen, reducing all the other actors to bit players who may as well be faceless. She is also at her sexiest, in a film which just before the Hollywood code came into order took advantage of the slack rules when it came to sexual suggestiveness and nudity - note the topless women being tortured and Dietrich's sex hungry performance as pre signs of a filmmaker running riot in a pre-prudish playground, given all the toys at his disposal.

The Scarlet Empress is viewed positively today by fans of Dietrich and von Sternberg, though some validly believe that the visuals took precedence over everything else. In his book on Marlene's film, Homer Dickens wrote, "Never before had there been such pomp and pageantry; all attention was geared to the visuals. Ferocious icons, ominous serfs, bells, cuckoo clocks, pillars, brought a Byzantine flavour to the surroundings, a kind of German expressionism."

Roger Ebert, writing a highly complimentary review of the film in 2005, agreed that there was a heck of a lot of style, but didn't believe it was bogged down by the visual obsessions. "Here is a film so crammed with style, so surrounded by it and weighted down with it, that the actors peer out from the display like children in a toy store. The film tells the story of Catherine the Great as a bizarre visual extravaganza, combining twisted sexuality and bold bawdy humour as if Mel Brooks had collaborated with the Marquis de Sade. As drama, The Scarlet Empress makes no sense, nor does it attempt to. This is not a resource for history class. Its primary subject is von Sternberg's erotic obsession with Dietrich, whom he objectified in a series of movies that made her face one of the immortal icons of the cinema. Whether she could act was beside the point for him; it would have been a distraction."

Writing about Marlene's performance, Dickens saw serious flaws. "Dietrich's performance, without proper translations, was good as could be expected under the circumstances. Her earlier sequences as the shy princess were near perfect, but when she later becomes the power within the palace, there was no believability."

Ebert however, giving the film 4 out of 4 stars, raved "When Dietrich is onscreen, however, nothing is too good for her; not only do von Sternberg's lighting and cinematography make her the centre and subject of every scene, but he devises extraordinary moments for as, as when, clad in a fur uniform and cape, with an improbable sable military hat, she mounts a horse and leads a cavalry charge up the grand staircase. 'It took more than one man to change my name to Shanghai Lily,' she says in Shanghai Express, but it only took von Sternberg to make her Marlene Dietrich." Clearly, Ebert "got" it.

Their final film together came in 1935 with the romantic drama The Devil is a Woman. A cold yet expertly delivered finale for the pair, it was a fitting swan song for a duo who had made some of the most striking and memorable movies of the early talkie period. While keeping the visual purity of the silent era, Sternberg and Dietrich used sound as a tool to merely enhance the image on screen. The Devil is a Woman, in my view not one of their best collaborations, remains sharp and precise all the same, portraying Dietrich as all women and von Sternberg as every longing male.

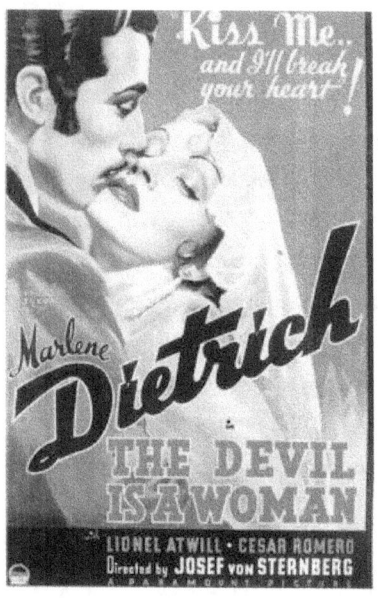

The Devil is a Woman was made at a changing time for the film business, in particular Paramount, who had been suffering from poor profits at the box office. Seeing as von Sternberg's films were seen as expensive extravagances, Paramount were only willing to indulge the filmmaker for so long. Proud for some time to be releasing films that offered more than standard thrills,

Paramount drew the line at films that made them little profit. Unfortunately, once The Devil is a Woman was released to little fan fare and underwhelming box office, his contract was finished. After seven films, it seemed as if the public had fallen out of love with Dietrich and von Sternberg's eccentric, stylised movies. Some reviewers however were still won over, with The New York Times calling it their best film together since The Blue Angel, though most found it lacklustre.

Variety however simply had to praise Dietrich. "Not even Garbo in the Orient has approached, for spectacular effects, Dietrich in Spain. Her costumes are completely incredible, but completely fascinating and suitable to The Devil is a Woman. They reek with glamour. Miss Dietrich emerges as a glorious achievement, a supreme consolidation of the sartorial, make-up and photographic arts."

Their relationship as filmmaker and star had begun with a bang, but ended with a whimper. The truth is though, that The Devil is a Woman has stood the test of time. It has little of the distracting subplots of their earlier films and is certainly more straight forward, if not harsher. This is not a schmaltzy parting of the ways, but a no nonsense split, a master of cinema bidding farewell to his beautiful muse through visual metaphors, his feeling veiled by cinematic stylisation. There is no moral message, no real heart to the picture, which could not have been more apt for a von Sternberg aware that the pair had run their course as a unit. "Dietrich and I have progressed as far as possible together, and my being with her will help neither her nor me," he said bluntly.

The unsettling part of the film is the fact that the two male leads look remarkably like Josef himself. When Alexander Walker brought this point up in an interview with von Sternberg, the director replied "Everyone in my films is like me... spiritually." Was The Devil is a Woman, with its von Sternberg doppelganger romantic lead, smooching passionately with Dietrich, his way of self inflicting a last masochistic punch in the gut?

Few at the time mourned the end of this collaboration, with Dietrich getting through a commercial down spell before regaining momentum as a screen star within a year or two. Sternberg though, was a little bitter, and displayed true arrogance when he later said, "No puppet in the history of the world has been submitted to as much manipulation as a leading lady of mine who, in seven films, not only had hinges and voice under control other than her own but the expression of her eyes and the nature of her thoughts."

He later also observed, "Miss Dietrich is me - I am Miss Dietrich!" Though his point is valid, and he very much did carve Dietrich into the woman he desired her to be, he too would have had nothing without her. To say he even led the way Dietrich thought may have been an overstatement, but von Sternberg was in part living out his own fantasy as puppet master in real life as well as on screen. He may have been slightly deluded or prone to overstating his egomaniacal power over Marlene, but it's a fact they both gained much from one another. It could also be said though that with Dietrich's exit von Sternberg lost much more than a mere puppet, but his livelihood, his commercial appeal and, perhaps worst of all, his muse.

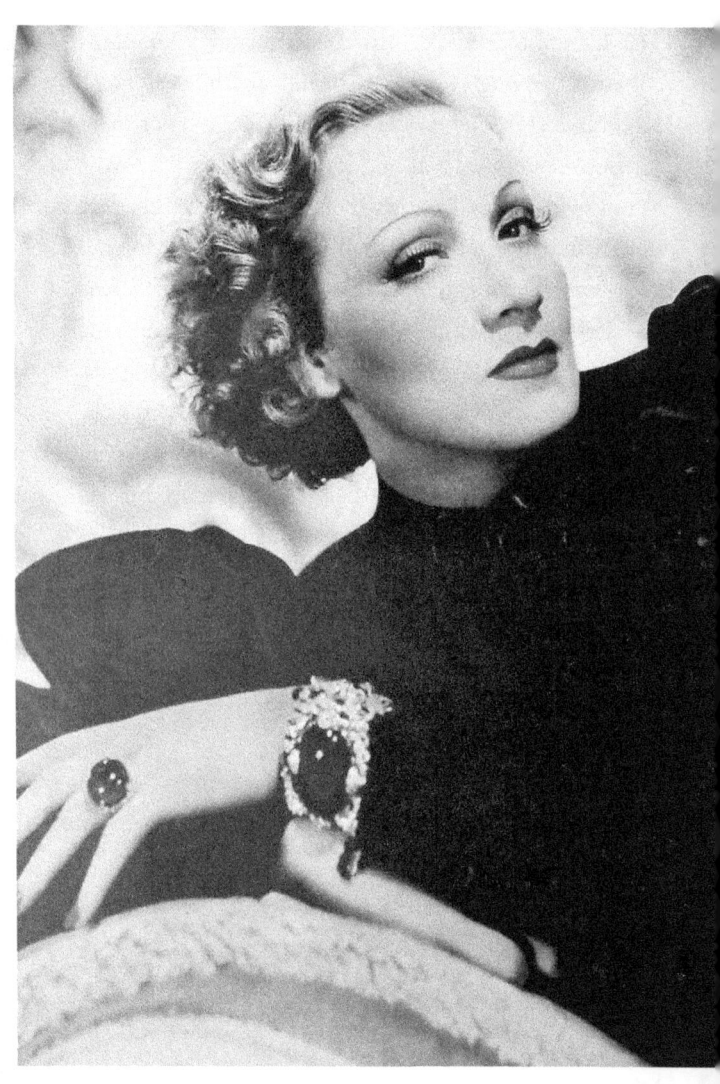

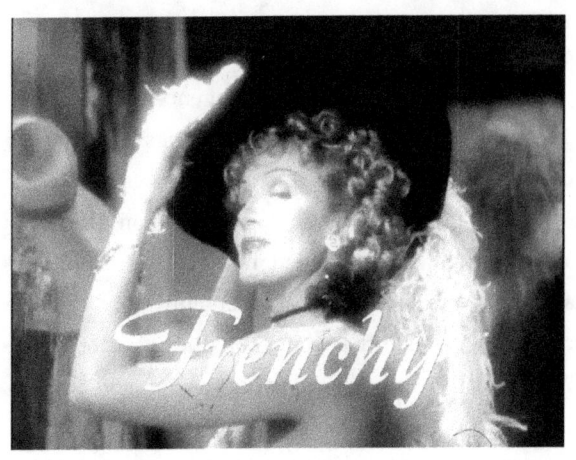

Freed from Bondage:
After the Collaboration

"Mother Theresa with better legs."
- Billy Wilder on Marlene Dietrich

"Shadow conceals—light reveals. To know what to reveal and what to conceal, and in what degrees to do this, is all there is to art." - Josef von Sternberg

"I am a teacher who took a beautiful woman, instructed her, presented her carefully," Sternberg later said, "edited her charms, disguised her imperfections and led her to crystallize a pictorial aphrodisiac. She was a perfect medium, who with intelligence absorbed my direction, and despite her own misgivings responded to my conception of a female archetype."

Though the theories relating to the von Sternberg and Dietrich movies thought up by critics and academics are interesting and certainly valid in some respects, I feel that some of the psychoanalytic dissection not only comes across as over studious, but threatens to take away the enjoyment from the films themselves. Reading a film is one thing, and can certainly be a rewarding and fulfilling task, but surely the main aim of film at its best is to entertain while hopefully informing and provoking thought. Let us not forget though, that in the days when Dietrich and von Sternberg's films were being released, film was not widely viewed as an art form, but as mere entertainment, often derogatorily deemed to be pure escapism at best and mindless drivel at worst. In his 1936 book, Keep the Aspidistra Flying, George Orwell comments on cinema from the viewpoint of the rather superior minded young writer Gordon Comstock, singling out not Dietrich but her so called rival Greta Garbo, when pointing out the mindlessness of the film experience. Of course, Dietrich herself saw film as both an artistic outlet and a good living, while von Sternberg, conscious of every visual opportunity, clearly saw it as a format equal to painted art and literature. In his films he evoked feelings, moods and emotions, and certainly did not view the cinema as purely entertainment. Like the greatest of early sound filmmakers, von Sternberg was preoccupied, while reluctantly hoping to please the studios, to make the viewer think as well as be moved and entertained. Though he clearly put across messages in his work, it is doubtful whether he would have been aware of half the theories written about by film academics and students.

In the book, In the Realm of Pleasure, Gaylyn Studlar pushes the fact that Dietrich and von Sternberg's films were largely perverted exercises in masochism. It is clear that there is a little bit of self torturing going on in many of these films, with the older von Sternberg placing himself, consciously or unconsciously, in the cuckolds. But the theories in the aforementioned text regarding Dietrich as an androgynous mother figure, a punisher, are somewhat far fetched, though they do make for good reading.

There is another way to view the collaboration. Though in the past Marlene was often seen as a mere toy in Josef's cinematic game, the beautiful puppet to his master, these days Dietrich is no longer the passive object in von Sternberg's stylised fetish fantasies. In fact, in the face of his shrunken worship, she is empowered as a proto feminist. Modern viewers see Dietrich as the dominant one and von Sternberg the desperate voyeur hiding behind filmmaking trickery. Though one has to draw the line at links to oedipal and castration theories, one can see there is a question of power here, with the balance tipping over into Dietrich's favour.

Dietrich's film career is defined by moments rather than films, but in all her 1930s movies every scene she has on screen is memorable, and in each one it is impossible to take your eyes off of her. Yet her best work is with Sternberg. In Dishonoured, her third film with Josef, she consolidated her fame and popularity with another fine turn as a female spy, in a film which seemed to fetishise Marlene even more. Clearly, von Sternberg was just as intoxicated by his goddess as the film going public. In my view, and the views of many others, Shanghai Express is the highlight of Dietrich and von Sternberg's collaboration, a strange and often surreal adventure drama set on a train that is taken over by rebels. Dietrich is the sultry Shanghai Lily, looking at her absolute best and delivering a charismatic turn that dominated the film despite her making very little effort, at least seemingly so.

By 1932 she was at her height. She was cool, suggestive, transgressive, light years ahead of her time in the way she fused sexuality, mystery and myth. At the same time, she was an adored star of the era and viewers felt like they knew her. She appeared in the press with her daughter and husband as if all was good in the Dietrich family home. Though behind closed doors their life was anything but ordinary, Dietrich played the PR game like a pro, clearing the way for generations of stars to follow, none of whom I might add could hope to match her appeal.

Released the same year as Shanghai Express was Blonde Venus, a close second in my view to being the ultimate Dietrich experience. In some ways Blonde Venus has Dietich at her best, and she expresses more range than she does in the other von Sternberg films, but for some reason the highly stylised Shanghai Express lingers longer in the mind.

As great as Dietrich was in von Sternberg's films, she was also very much limited by whatever the director had in his mind, and what parts of his fantasies he was able to put on screen. Boxed into his fetishes, Dietrich became an item of titillation, an ideal, still empowered but ultimately limited as an actress. As soon as she was free from von Sternberg, when the pair knew their collaboration had gone as far as it could, she was able to stretch herself. Though she always linked to those films, she often distanced herself from the characters, stating they were not her, and that the image of Dietrich was one created from all her parts, with a bit of the real self in there for good measure. The Dietrich of post-Sternberg was still a figure of glamour, though she could also loosen her bullets too. She made Desire in 1936, a film she often called her personal favourite, or more to the point the only film she need not be ashamed of. There were commercial misfires, such as Angel (1937) for Paramount Pictures, but she won the world over alongside James Stewart in Destry Rides Again (1939), a charming western with her at her comic best. Pure charisma, she stole the film from under Stewart's nose. Intentional or not, Marlene walked away with the picture.

As late as Orson Welles' masterpiece Touch of Evil, released in 1958 when Dietrich was in her fifties and already setting out her new career as a globe trotting cabaret singer, she was still giving movies a needed dose of glamour, some old fashioned sex appeal and other worldly appeal. Yet in her latter years as a singer and performer, entertaining millions the world over, she could not have been further from von Sternberg's limited idea of her as every woman. Still, she excelled in the aftermath of their collaboration, spreading her wings and escaping his cage of infatuation.

Though always a skilled filmmaker, Josef von Sternberg failed to recapture the world's imaginations as he had with Marlene after they parted ways. Now remembered mostly for his iconic films with her, he is often viewed as a semi tragic figure, the man who wanted his star so badly but was never able to obtain her; how true this is, of course, is up to debate.

Dietrich's most important role came during the Second World War when she devoted herself to entertaining the allied troops. Her work during the conflict, raising moral of soldiers, many injured and missing their home lives, with Dietrich touring and performing tirelessly, earned her the Medal of Freedom in 1947. Inevitably, anything that came after was bound to be a let down, and Dietrich soon tired of the movies, appearing in less and less films as the years went on. Still, Dietrich retained her glamour. Famously bendable when it came to her sexuality, she was also an icon of style. Asked about her clothing, often controversial, she famously and defiantly replied, "I dress for the image.

Not for myself, not for the public, not for fashion, not for men. If I dressed for myself I wouldn't bother at all. Clothes bore me. I'd wear jeans. I adore jeans. I get them in a public store – men's, of course; I can't wear women's trousers. But I dress for the profession."

The next phase in Dietrich's life, and certainly the part she seems to have enjoyed the most, was her new life as a cabaret performer. From the fifties to the mid seventies when she retired, she toured the world singing songs and entertaining fans in every corner of the globe. Burt Bacharach has been her musical guide during the mid 1950s, and like she needed von Sternberg in the movies, she needed Bacharach when it came to the music. When Bacharach left to focus on song writing, she felt like she had lost her maestro. Yet on and on she continued, the illusion becoming more carefully worked out as the years went by. Through delicate lighting, the right posture and costumes, not to mention the obligatory tape to pull back her face, the Dietrich myth moved on into new eras, never seeming to date or tire. It wasn't until bad health and pain forced her to quit that she retreated from the world's view. During a stage performance in 1975 she fell and broke her thigh, and with her legs being her two most valuable assets, she knew she only had one option.

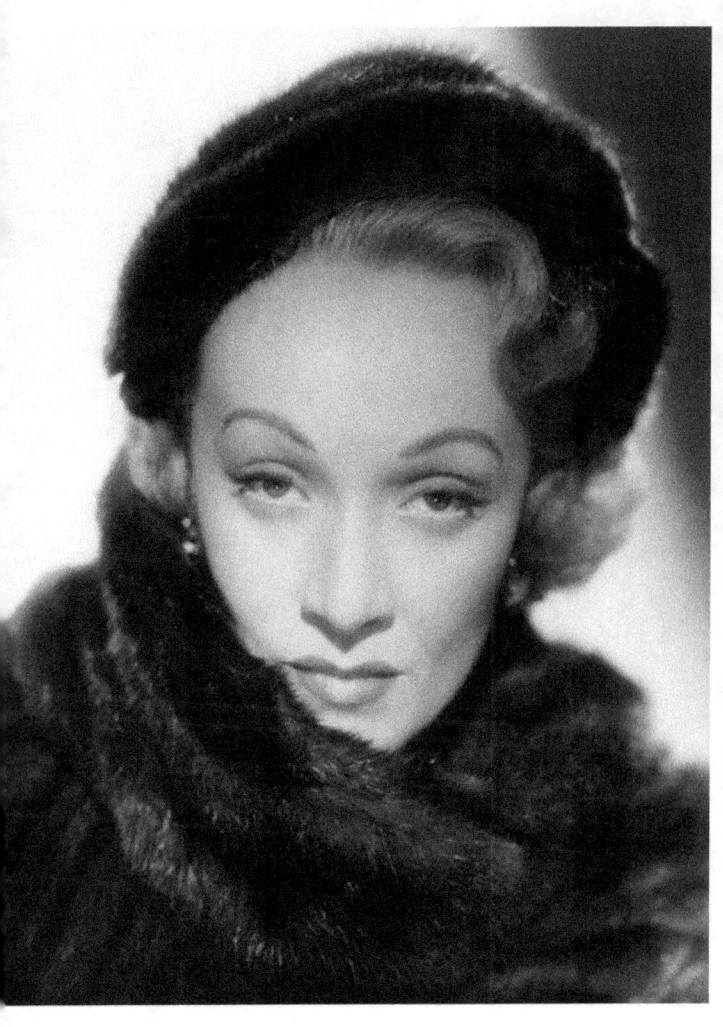

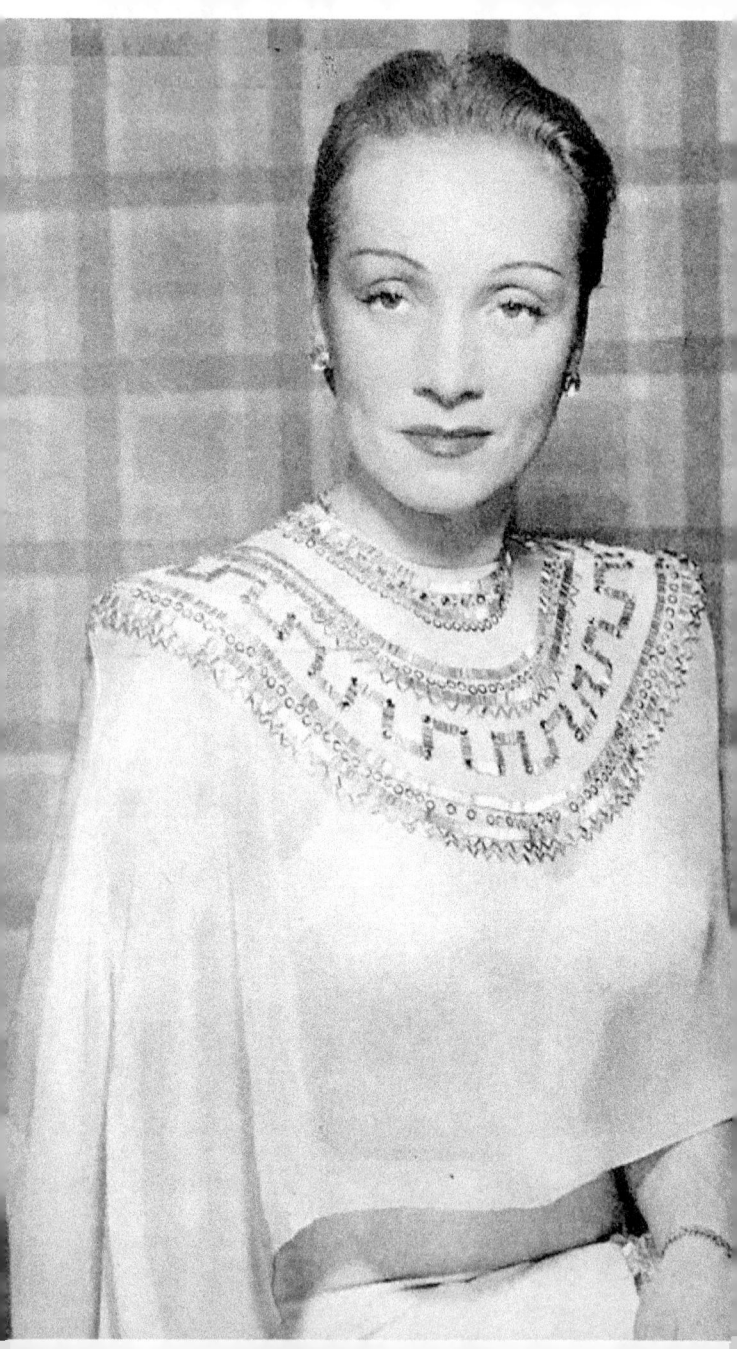

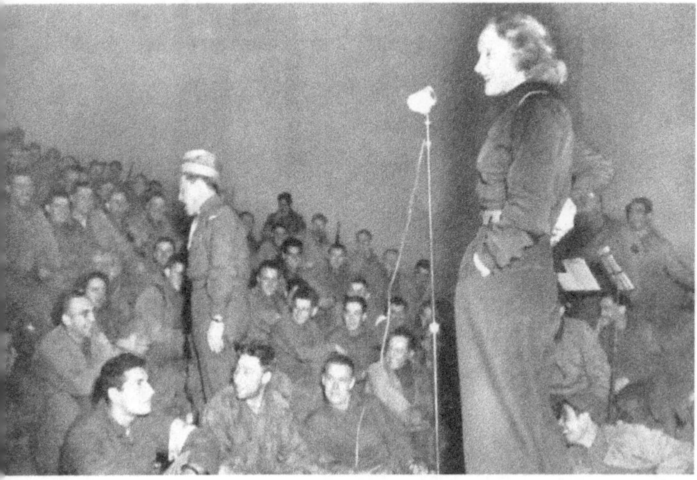

Dietrich and the troops...

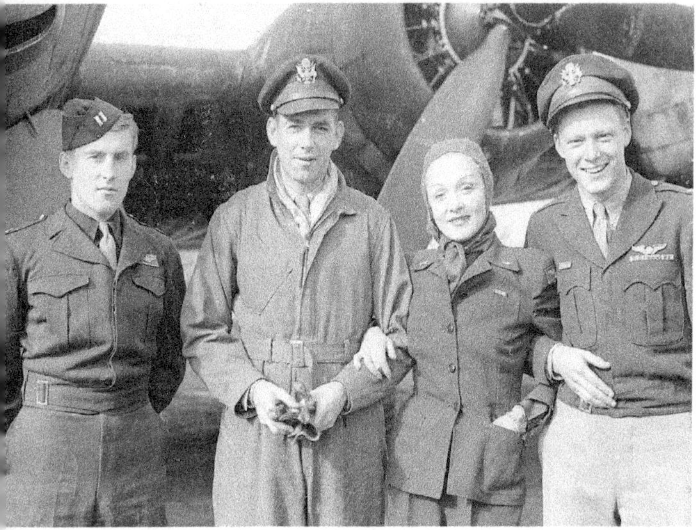

She spent most of her final years in her Paris apartment, seeing friends and writing her memoir. Few pictures have been shown from the final seventeen years of her life, meaning that the aged, ailing Dietrich is a thing of the imagination and all we have are the films, the records, the stunning photographs, all featuring Dietrich in her prime. The myth is alive and well, but only because Marlene knew when to bow out.

As a result, many people now know Dietrich for her personality, and may be totally unaware of the enjoyable filmography she left behind. There are lost gems in there, like Witness to the Prosecution and Alfred Hitchcock's Stage Fright, a film which she walks away with, wonderfully playing a variation of her vampish image. It's a varied filmography for sure, starting in the pre-sound twenties in Europe and ending, poignantly, in the later 1970s with a cameo in David Hemmings' Just A Gigolo. These days, a person's fame too often takes precedence over the work that made them famous in the first place. I feel this has happened with Dietrich. Though Marlene was in many ways, and still is, an idea, a commodity, even a package - she was basically selling herself as the product - it's her films which we should really look to if we are to grasp the sheer magnitude of her myth. Photographs may remain striking, audio recordings charming, but the films give us the larger than life Dietrich, in all her glory, preserved forever. While we may wonder what was so good about stars who existed before the advent of film, thankfully we have a whole canon of Dietrich delights to feast upon.

To say Dietrich's fame was just down to her films though, would be foolish. She was a myth in her own life time, and though she denied this, it was an enigma she created herself. "I am not a myth" she once famously said, though the fact she was addressing the issue suggests she knew she really was one. When Dietrich said those words, her career was definitely far from over. Her life in the movies was limited to a cameo now and then, but she was still a formidable and hugely popular entertainer, touring the globe with her singing act. She was still vital, out there in world at an age when most people are in the rocking chair. For Marlene to admit she was mythical was to say she was but a face from the past, a nostalgic figure from Hollywood's bygone era. Now of course, with Dietrich gone, she really is a myth.

Marlene Dietrich is the embodiment of the star who existed for her public, the celebrity who kept the image and myth alive to the final day. Dietrich the woman and Dietrich the star may have been two very different people, though undoubtedly given the ego of the star these two entities will have overlapped frequently, especially towards the end when Dietrich was a living legend, denying her own myth yet also enhancing it with her reclusive lifestyle. But it was more than stardom that kept Dietrich mounting the stage steps for the paying punters until the day she could no longer do it. It was her art, her creativity, Dietrich as a being, an entity and an idea which the public were ever hungry for. They kept buying the ticket, and expressing a desire to do so - so Marlene, until the fateful day came when she could no longer fulfill her demand, kept giving them what they wanted.

To Dietrich, being an artist was something to be proud of, and she clearly saw actors as artists too, if not of the caliber of writers and painters. Still, in later life it was clear she was glad she had partaken in the world of the imagination, the movies and the stage, where dreams come to life and are fulfilled. Of artists, an older Dietrich wrote: "They are a race completely apart from all other human beings. Their emotions, all their feelings, their reactions are opposed to so-called "normal" people's sentiments. They are vulnerable and deeply sensitive people, due to their talents, their super-imagination, their knowledge of hidden influences of which we ordinary human beings are not. They are not easy to live with – if you choose to live with them at all, if you have the luck to meet them at all. Writers, composers, painters – also artists like directors and actors fall into the same category. They have to be handled with kid-gloves, mentally and physically. All their reactions go to extremes, compared to non-artistic human beings. As I was lucky enough to meet and love and work for many, many artists, I learned, not without heartbreak and pain, to become a better, more intelligent, respectful and devoted person. No tears were wasted in the process. My tears – not theirs."

Dietrich was 90 at the time she died in 1992 of renal failure, and had been ailing for years, slowly crumbling away like rocks on a sea front. To Dietrich, the crashing waves were time. And there was the world outside, the intrusive cameras of the press, the reaching hands of the people who loved her and yearned for one more glance. She kept the image alive until the end by concealing the inevitability of time, the sad reality of age. She's forever Marlene.

And Marlene's legacy is in the films, most of all her work with von Sternberg. Whether we view the von Sternberg-Dietrich collaborations as pure escapism, or cloaked psycho-sexual curios masquerading as sleek slices of cinema, it doesn't really matter, because the movies themselves remain special, unique and in a world of their very own. Often dreamlike, they transcend reality while never seeming totally ridiculous or unbelievable. Dietrich shines brightly in them all, and von Sternberg challenges the viewer into mentally dissecting every angle, every shot, every cinematic choice. Marlene is his goddess throughout the varied adventures, the shady goings on and the often delightfully seedy scenarios, never failing to embody whatever was lingering in his mind or weighing down his mentality. She was his obsession, and for a while she was one of cinema and the world's great obsessions. She glowed brightly again in movies after working with von Sternberg, but it was never quite the same; and as much as she would have hated to admit it, she knew this fact too.

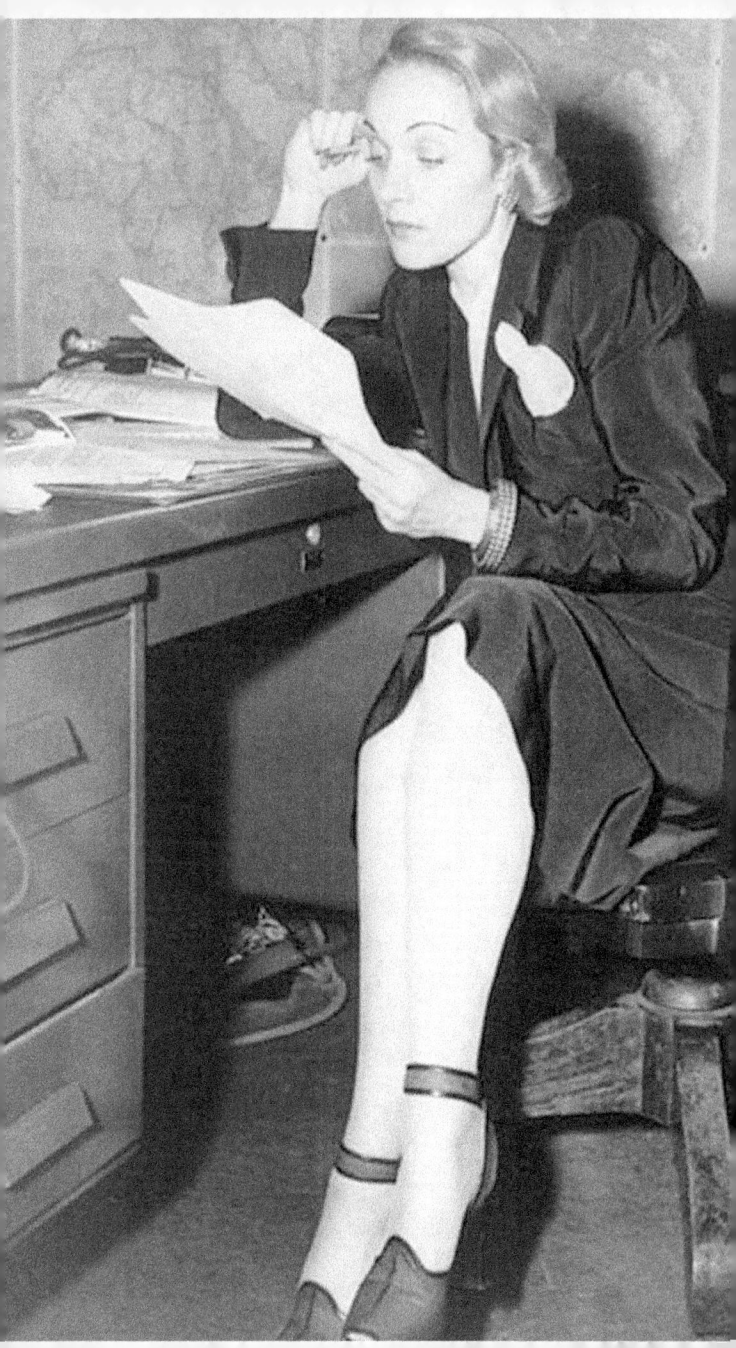

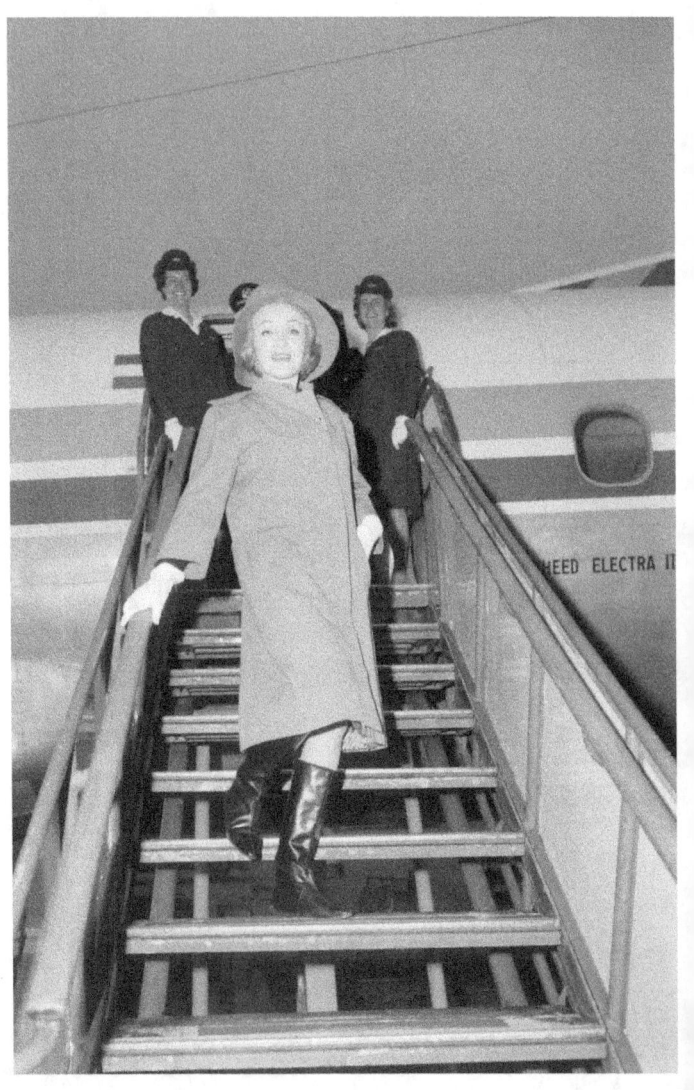

References

The following sources were useful in the completion of this book;

Books

Dietrich, by Alexander Walker

Movie Icons: Marlene Dietrich

Marlene Dietrich, by Charlotte Chandler

Marlene Dietrich, by Maria Riva

Marlene Dietrich: Life and Legend, by Stephen Bach

My Life, by Marlene Dietrich

The Phenomenology of Spectacle, by James Phillips

The Films of Marlene Dietrich, by Homer Dickens

Newspapers, magazines and websites;

New York Times

The Observer/Guardian

Sense of Cinema

Criterion

Birth, Movies, Death

Roger Ebert.com

ABOUT CHRIS WADE

Chris Wade is a UK based writer, filmmaker and musician. As well as running the acclaimed music project Dodson and Fogg, he has written books on The Kinks, Malcolm McDowell, Captain Beefheart, Robert De Niro and many others. He has also released audiobooks of his comedic fiction, such as Cutey and the Sofaguard, narrated by Rik Mayall. His other projects include Hound Dawg Magazine, for which he has interviewed such people as Sharon Stone, Donovan and Jethro Tull's Ian Anderson. His art films include The Apple Picker (winning Best Film at the Sydney World Film Festival, and featuring Toyah Willcox and Nigel Planer), and he's made documentaries on George Melly, Lindsay Anderson, Charlie Chaplin and Orson Welles.

More info at his website:
wisdomtwinsbooks.weebly.com